MW00914449

LIVING

~~IN~~

WITH

FEAR

(A Quest for Survival)

J. I. GRANVILLE

Copyright © 2019 J. I. Granville
All rights reserved
First Edition

PAGE PUBLISHING, INC.
Conneaut Lake, PA

First originally published by Page Publishing 2019

No part of this publication may be copied or distributed, transmitted, transcribed, stored in a retrieval system or translated into any human or computer language, in any form by means electronic, mechanical, magnetic, manual or otherwise. It may not be disclosed to third parties without the express written permission of the author, J.I. Granville.

ISBN 978-1-64544-909-6 (pbk)
ISBN 978-1-64701-719-4 (hc)
ISBN 978-1-64544-910-2 (digital)

Printed in the United States of America

My minister once preached that no child is competent until he/she has grasped the meaning of his/her parents' experiences. With that in mind, I tell our story so that our grandchildren might understand.

Thank you Matt Greenia. You made my
idea for the front cover a reality.

Dear Reader,

This memoir provides an exploration into the lives of a police officer and his family—my family. During your journey, you will witness a phenomenon—the conscription of the recruit's family. They are inadvertently inducted into the world of the Blue Brotherhood. There they encounter battlefields, traverse terrain, endure pitfalls, conquer peaks and enjoy plateaus.

Adversaries are diverse, but the most pernicious foe is **FEAR** of injury and of death. Those who live **in** fear succumb. Those who learn to live **with** the fear survive.

My diary, police reports, newspaper articles and court transcripts serve as affidavits about our twenty-four-year tour of duty.

Each encounter is truly depicted, but names have been changed to protect confidentiality.

Enjoy your excursion,
J. I. Granville

CONTENTS

PROLOGUE

The probability of injury and the possibility of death are constant fears. But a police wife must not allow her fear to go unchecked. For her own sanity, she must cope. So I did. I reminded myself of the advice that had been given at our orientation meeting. All the cadets' wives, fiancées and girlfriends had listened intently as the lieutenant issued this good advice: "Do not purchase a radio to monitor police calls. You can die a thousand deaths by listening to your loved one calling out a pursuit or yelling for backup. It will torture you with unnecessary worry. Start to worry only if you receive a phone call from the hospital." Even though I wanted to hear my husband in action, I determined not to die those thousand unnecessary deaths. I did not buy a police band radio. Instead, I waited for Mike to get home. Then I would wheedle every detail! Somehow the knowledge of the good he was doing made my fretting bearable.

Within weeks, my rookie husband came home very late one night. His eyes were bloodshot, and his face was red. I immediately attributed his physical state to after-hours drinking with the Brotherhood, and I warned him not to fall into that pit. He informed me that his condition was due to tear gas! Summer rioting had begun.

The next day, I watched as he prepared to leave the house with additional equipment. Along with the usual gun belt and bulletproof vest, he was carrying a riot helmet with a visor and a long wooden baton. I was a nervous wreck. I reminded him to be extra careful, and I even gave him an extra kiss. Within minutes after his departure, I heard his car coming back up the driveway. I met him at the back door. "I have to know you're all right with this," he said. "If my mind is on you when I'm out in the street, I won't be able to concentrate on my job." He did not have to say the rest, *Then I will get killed.* For his sake, I forced an encouraging smile, "I'm okay. Go." As he once again backed down the driveway, I turned away, took a deep breath and willed the fear to the back of my mind. There it lingered silently until the first hospital call. Little did I know how many more calls would come.

Over the years, Mike sustained several police injuries, and each raised my level of anxiety. It was his twelfth year on the force when I experienced the horrible anguish felt only by others who have lost a soul mate. Before leaving for work, Mike had told me that Squad B (4:00 PM to midnight shift) would be having a farewell gathering for their unit commander after work. Captain Ben was leaving them, and the guys had all chipped in to buy him a plaque, which proclaimed, "To the Best Boss, From the Best Squad."

Today, the captain was either going to be buried in the booking department by a vindictive chief or appointed the new Chief of Police. In either case, his men would no longer enjoy direct contact with him. The eleven o'clock news confirmed the captain's promotion, so I knew there would be a celebration!

My diary entry reveals my horror:

> *The sky is no longer black. It is taking on the gray of 4:00 AM, and through the open bedroom window there is still no sound of an approaching car. In my mind was a too vivid recollection of a previous incident. Then, it had*

taken authorities six hours to notify me of Mike's injury. Should I call the department? No, that would embarrass him.

4:15 AM: What am I worrying about? He's probably having a great time! Stop tormenting yourself. Go to sleep. There is only two hours left on my alarm clock.

5:00 AM: The dog's barking awoke me. Someone was gently knocking at the back door. The peep-hole revealed a uniformed police officer. His head was bent, and his face was out of view. With trepidation I open the door. The uniform belonged to Mike's partner, a very good friend. Tom's eyes were swollen and helplessly blank. As he tried to speak, lines appeared on his forehead which indicated his pain.

"Is he dead?" I whispered. Tom's head nodded affirmatively as his arms reached out to me. For mini seconds my body stood paralyzed, yet my mind was racing. God, how many times have I wondered how it would happen; where I would be, and how I would get the news? I've anticipated this scene on so many previous occasions, I should be prepared for this! I took a deep breath and sternly reminded myself, "Keep control. All cops' wives are expected to be strong!" But Tom's silent tears broke all my delusions of strength, and I went into his arms. Holding each other, we cried together.

Minutes became illusive and some time passed before I felt the warm masculine hand gently messaging my back. Tender words entered *my ears, "Shh, shh. Honey don't cry. **What's wrong?"***

*My eyes flew open! "Mike!" I gasped. My incredulous surprise instantly turned into rage which was vented with my screeching rebuke, "Damn you! You could have called!" Relief allowed my arms to release the damp pillow and fly around his neck. The strength of his embrace reassured me that **this was real**. The other had been a terrible nightmare!*

After calming me, Mike explained that he had not wanted to awaken me with a phone call. Then and there, I made him promise that he would call at any hour of the night—not to wake me, but to allow me to sleep.

CHAPTER 1

Unsuspecting Wife

How did I ever become a police wife? I did not marry a cop. My life was fairly normal. According to my birth certificate, I was born a fraternal twin, but Barbara and I look identical. We share a brother, eight years our senior. Because of the age gap, Paul always seemed to be away: a college student, an Air Force lieutenant and a NASA space engineer.

When my father was a young man, he and four brothers built Gee Bee airplanes. At the 1932 National Air Race, Jimmy Doolittle won the world land speed record in the Gee Bee no. 11. During World War II, Dad used his welding skills to rebuild damaged aircraft. Later he worked in the helicopter industry.

My mother, a blue-collar worker, sewed everything from Carter underwear to Spaulding baseballs. For many years, Mom volunteered as a Sunday school supervisor and a Girl Scout leader. Those nonpaying jobs were her most rewarding. She was an intuitive person and realized that the constant comparison between her twins was unhealthy. She stopped dressing us alike at a young age, argued with the school to put us into separate classrooms and baked two individual birthday cakes. She wanted us to consider ourselves as individuals, not as a set. Just one month after our twelfth birthdays, she died from complications incurred after colon surgery. My father was left with three children to raise on his own.

By the time Barbara and I entered high school, we were self-assured and had developed our own personalities. Since comparisons were no longer intimidating, we occasionally dressed alike. We enjoyed confusing people, but sometimes having a double was complicated. For instance, whenever a stranger approached, I would have to determine if that person was a friend of my sister. If the engaging person was Barbara's acquaintance, I would have to convince that person that I was June, her twin. I cannot tell you how many times I have said, "I am not Barbara."

Because we both took college-prep classes, it was inevitable that we would be assigned to at least one classroom together. There, alphabetical order placed Barbara at the last desk in one row and me at the front desk in the next row. Throughout the entire year, our teacher was in awe because our test scores were exactly alike! If any question was missed, it would always be the same one. Mrs. Fipps was sure that we were perfect examples of twins who could communicate through mental telepathy! Of course, we allowed her to believe that we were exceptional—until the end of the year. Then we enlightened her with a logical explanation. We studied her course together; therefore, we were either strong or weak in the same areas. I think we burst her bubble!

Throughout high school, we were extremely active. We remained on the honor roll, and we performed in majorettes. I was president of the student council, and my sister was the judge on the student court. Learning from my mother's fine example, I also did volunteer work. I chaperoned younger teens at the community center every Friday night. Saturdays were catch-up for housework, which Barbara and I equally shared. To earn spending money, I worked an eight-hour shift every Sunday waiting tables at a small restaurant. During my sophomore year of high school, I began to reserve Saturday and Sunday evenings for Mike.

We met when a mutual friend arranged a double blind date for Barbara and me. Mike and his friend had already graduated from a high school in a neighboring city. Mike, age eighteen, was just home from a six-month tour in the Coast Guard. My father did not know that, and Mike did not know that I was only fifteen! On our fourth date, Mike asked my age. He almost choked on his coffee, but he did arrange for a fifth date before leaving me that night. We continued to date steadily for the next two and a half years. By working two jobs, Mike was able to give me a very special high school graduation present, a diamond engagement ring. Because we were both anxious to get married, I declined the opportunity to attend a two-year nursing school. Instead, I entered a one-year dental assistant's school. In April 1962, I celebrated two happy occasions: my capping ceremony and a small family wedding.

After graduation, I immediately took the full-time position offered by the dentist with whom I had served my apprenticeship. Mike found a better job—driving a Pepsi-Cola delivery truck. Since Mike was obligated to attend Coast Guard meetings one night a week, my father accepted an open dinner invitation every Wednesday evening. The arrangement was delightful. I always looked forward to his company, and Dad definitely enjoyed my home-cooked meals.

On hot summer nights, Mike and I escaped the heat of our fourth-floor walk-up apartment by going to an air-conditioned movie. Apartment dwelling was a new experience for me. I had spent my entire life in the same small single-family home. Walking to work was another new experience. Mike and I shared a 1957 Chevy, which he took to work (a farther distance away) while I walked a mile (downhill) to the inner-city dental office each morning. I rode the bus back up the steep hill each night.

After one and a half years of blissful privacy, Dad suggested we move in with him so that we could save enough money to buy our own house. One day, severe cramps forced me to leave work early. I was very concerned because I was one-and-a-half months pregnant. After an episode in the bathroom, I called my doctor. The next day, he decided that I was probably still carrying the fetus. But at my three-month checkup, the obstetrician declared that I was not progressed enough to be three months along. He now believed that I initially miscarried and then immediately became pregnant again. This news was a relief. I had been secretly worrying that something may be wrong with our first baby. Now I joyfully started counting all over again. My diary states: *I'll never be 112 pounds again! I'm so large that people suspect twins, but an ultrasound assures a single birth. Not only has the original due date passed, the second due date passed two weeks ago! People think I'm seeking a world's record. It's been almost eleven months since our first announcement. Everyone has been waiting a long time!*

Because I was so late, I experienced a "dry birth". As if twenty-one hours of labor was not bad enough, the doctor was late returning to the hospital for the delivery. By the time he arrived, the large head of my nine-pound, two-ounce baby boy had already caused a tearing, which required many sutures. But at the moment of delivery, all concern was centered upon Lonny. He was blue and not breathing! He had been strangled by his own umbilical cord. Fortunately, resuscitation revived him quickly so there was no brain damage. After a year of nausea, I was finally a MOM!

When Lonny was six months old, we moved into a fixer-upper Cape-style home. Lonny was cranky with roseola on moving day! Thank God for my father. He was always willing to babysit on any needed occasion. With his help, I was able to return to dental assisting on Saturdays. To make up for the rest of my lost salary, Mike worked an extra weekend job.

I was eight months pregnant with our second child when Lonny (not quite two) needed immediate surgery. My husband and I were directed to the waiting room, where Mike wiped my tears and tried to comfort me. He assured me, "It's much easier for Lonny to have a hernia operation now, than when he's older. He's so young, he won't even remember it." But no matter what Mike said, I could not dispel the horrible image of my son's petrified face pushed up against the bars of a pediatric cage (crib). One of his little arms was reaching out to me while the other clung to his teddy bear. His screams echoed down the hallway, chasing after me as I abandoned him.

A month later, Lonny was swinging from his backyard jungle gym when I left for the hospital again. This time, I would be the patient. Our second child was also two weeks late, but this time, the doctor was going to puncture my placenta to expedite the birth. While this delivery was not as horrific as the first, I did experience one complication. During labor, the baby had turned, so the obstetrician had to rotate her back into the proper birthing position. It seemed to take an eternity before Lori (nine-pound, one-ounce) was born. I decided that birthing was my last!

Happy family life continued. At age twenty-three, Mike switched to Coca-Cola. He received commendations for salesmanship, and he was now earning such good money that I enjoyed being a full-time housewife and mother. I also found time for college classes. For several semesters, Mike babysat while I attended one evening class a week.

Never did I suspect that my husband sought more in his life as well. Unknown to me was the discord arising from new ownership of the soda franchise. Mike was no longer happy at his job, and he was secretly thinking about other options. Amazingly, his new career was chosen because of a game! An old high school buddy had asked Mike to join his football team and play in the park department's Over-Twenty-Five Touch Football League. Most of the team were police officers. Mike joined up, and every Sunday, I would bundle the children for a park outing to watch the game. Even then, I was not aware of what he was contemplating. Nor did I know that the minor injuries sustained while playing on that police team would be a prelude to the more serious injuries he would receive once on the **real police team**!

CHAPTER 2

A Verbal Portrait

Michael was the eldest of three sons, born to a working-class American family, whose maternal lineage originated in Russia. Paternal ancestry hailed from England and Ireland. His name-sake was Uncle Michael, a Navy man, who went down with the USS *Bonefish* submarine during World War II. Mike's mother worked full-time, first in a bread factory, then in the meat department of a large grocery store chain. His father was a supervisor in an electrical factory and worked an extra weekend job, picking farm produce. He often took his oldest boy with him. At age seven, Mike picked string beans. At ten, he "topped" apple trees. (Boys picked what could not be reached by adults on ladders. They were the perfect size for the job—big enough to climb to the top, but not so big that they would damage the branches.) During adolescence, he played hooky from Russian language classes to play basketball. At age fourteen, his mother signed papers allowing him to work his summers under the hot tents of tobacco fields. This continued until he was old enough (age sixteen) to work at a local grocery store. Mike's father became ill, and Mike's wages were needed to pay the rent. Since he worked full-time while attending high school, he was unable to participate in any high school sports. Enjoyment had to be found during nonworking hours, so he joined the church choir and sang in two high school musicals. At age seventeen, Mike graduated from a public high school, which was well-known for its mathematics program. Although Mike excelled, college was out of the question because all of Mike's earnings had gone to support his family. Instead, he enlisted in the Coast Guard and served six months of active duty in a shore patrol unit. This program allowed young men to complete their service obligation by serving in a reserve unit for six and a half more years. During this time, Mike would have to attend meetings one night a week and go to training camp for two weeks every summer. Eventually, Mike was honorably discharged as a First Class Petty Officer.

A friend from his church was a neighbor of mine, and she was responsible for our introduction. During a double blind date, I was partnered with his best friend, and my twin sister was coupled with Mike. On the next double date, we swapped. Fate took its course, and Mike continued to date me. I may have been two and a half years younger by age, but I was mature because of my mother's early death.

While waiting for me to finish high school, Mike worked two jobs. He was twenty-one when he gave me a diamond engagement ring. Mike found better employment as a truck driver for Pepsi-Cola. At age twenty-four, he became a father, and he found more lucrative work with Coca-Cola. For several years, Mike won awards as a top salesman, but he became disenchanted with the new franchise owner. Now twenty-eight, he was the father of one son and one daughter. He had a family, a home mortgage and car payments.

Mike also had a great desire for a new occupation. He placed applications at two nearby police departments. It was months before he was finally scheduled to take their written exams, and months after that, the first city arranged an appointment for a verbal exam (a board review). Having passed that, the police department sent a recruitment sergeant to interview me. I apparently "passed muster" by affirming that I had no objection to Mike's career move. I assured, "I am happy to be a housewife. Mike earns the money which supports our family, so he has the right to be happy with his work." (I did not mention that I would have to go back to work to make up for the pay discrepancy.) The next step was a thorough physical examination. Mike flunked! Albumin in his urine indicated an infection in his system. Lonny had recently been very ill with scarlet fever, so it was assumed that Mike was in the early stages of "strep". The police physician gave him a prescription for antibiotics and told him to drink plenty of water until his next urine sample was tested. In April 1970, he finally entered the police academy at the elderly age of thirty. He went to class during the day and babysat at night, while I waited tables to make up for some of our lost income. On June 12, 1970, at 1300 hours (1:00 PM), I witnessed the official swearing-in ceremony. Mike, the oldest in the class, graduated fifth of twenty-eight finishing cadets. **He was a police officer! I was a cop's wife!**

CHAPTER 3

Unprepared

Mike entered the Field Service Division. He was a "street cop" dressed in a uniform and operating a cruiser. We immediately encountered our first problem—adjusting to a miserable work schedule. Patrolmen were required to rotate shifts every month. One month, Mike worked days (A-Squad); the next month was evenings (B-Squad); followed by a month on "dog watch" (C-Squad, midnight to 8:00 AM). Just as one became acclimated to one schedule, it was time to readjust. As if this were not enough to juggle, officers also rotated days off! First, it would be Monday/Tuesday; next it would be Tuesday/Wednesday; and so it went. This meant the family rarely enjoyed a normal weekend. Awaiting the rotation to Saturday/Sunday seemed to take forever. Hardest of all was the loss of almost every holiday!

Mike's crazy schedule made it impossible for me to keep my waitressing job, so he had to work extra shifts. At least one day a week, he worked a "private job" at the civic center, a construction site, in a lounge, or guarding a distinguished visitor. He was spending so much time on the job that I was becoming the primary caregiver for our children.

Eventually, Mike freed our family from the stressful rotation schedule by volunteering for the Task Force. Members of this special unit were guaranteed a permanent shift (6:00 PM to 2:00 AM) and one weekend day every week! But even this work was somewhat sporadic. Because the unit was designed to cope with peak hours and high crime, Mike was engaged in a lot of activity! Often, mandatory overtime or emergency "call-back" was required.

Somehow, Mike found the time to further educate himself so that he could better serve the city's 500,000 commuters and 160,000 residents. During his career, he attended as many schools and seminars as possible. His studies included homicide, arson, burglary, intelligence, sexual assaults, search and seizure, child abuse, EMS-MRT (Emergency Medical Service-Medical Response Team), photography, fingerprint classification, crime scene scrutiny and NCIC (National Crime Information Center) certification. In 1977, Mike obtained an Associate's Degree in criminal justice.

This extensive preparation was inadequate! There was no course for family survival techniques. We were not prepared for the many unknown hazards. Therefore, we had to find our own way of coping with each ominous ordeal. To fully understand, I must take you back to the beginning of Mike's police career.

CHAPTER 4

Assault in the Second Degree (1971)

It was December 1971. Mike had been on the job for a year and a half when he sustained his first serious injury. The arrest warrant was approved by Circuit Court 14. Mike's assailant was charged with Assault in the Second Degree, Reckless Driving and two counts of Violation of Mechanical Signal. While the episode was just another incident listed on the repeat offender's "RAP sheet" (Record of Arrest and Prosecutions), it would be the event that changed Mike's life forever.

At approximately 10:50 PM, Mike's partner ran into a coffee shop and returned to the cruiser with two steaming cups. Heat was needed to ease the frigid winter chill, and the caffeine was needed to keep alert for the last hour and ten minutes of their shift. Mike pulled the line-unit off the street, backing it up against an alley wall. Parked in that position, they would be safe from any surprises from the rear as they watched the busiest intersection in their district. They had only been parked a few minutes when a 1969 black Cadillac (repair plate RB...) came zooming up Allen Avenue. The car flew west through the red light at the intersection.

In that district, many people drove in such a manner, but this car was particularly interesting. It was the middle of winter.

All the windows were down, and the driver was wearing only a short-sleeve T-shirt! Officer Edgar immediately identified the driver as a well-known criminal. "That's Vern. He's probably high." This seemed a logical hypothesis since he had been previously arrested for possession and currently seemed impervious to the temperature. It was only nine degrees!

As Mike threw the shifting lever into drive, he facetiously responded, "Or maybe the windows are all broken." During a short chase, the accused not only ran the red light at Grant Street but showed complete disregard for the persons and property at the Vine Street intersection as well. When the maniac was forced to pull over, Mike approached the vehicle upon the driver's side while his partner took the appropriate position on the opposite side. Mike asked for his license. Vern produced a license belonging to a man named Karl, his lookalike brother. Impersonation was useless. Mike could tell the difference between the two and so informed the man. The driver insisted he was the man on the license, and that Vern was his twin brother. Hearing that statement, Officer Edgar started around the rear of the car so that he could approach the driver's side to confirm Mike's identification. As he was doing so, Mike asked the driver to shut his engine off. Instead of reaching for the key, Vern reached for the shifting lever. At that point, Mike had no doubt that the subject intended to drive away to prevent being arrested. Mike reached into the Cadillac with the intent of throwing the lever back into park and extracting the car keys from the ignition. *Why not try, it had worked before!*

Unfortunately, it did not work this time! During the struggle for the shifting lever, Vern successfully manipulated the electric windows. One locked upon Mike's arm. Vern then accelerated, driving away with the rookie running alongside. As Vern increased his speed, Mike could no longer keep up. He was being dragged! Mike yelled, "My arm's caught!"

Vern answered, "Fuck you!"

Then he steered his vehicle toward an oncoming car. The unsuspecting motorist quickly veered as far to his right as possible but was unable to completely miss Mike's body. The contact jarred Mike loose and propelled him along the frozen pavement! When his perpetual rolling finally stopped, Mike just lay there. Shallow breaths began to enter his lungs, and strange sounds filled his ears. His groggy brain recognized them. It was laughter! Exiting bar patrons had enjoyed the spectacle.

While Mike's back and leg injuries were being treated in the emergency room, his partner went to the detective division. He picked out a police photo of Vern and verified his date of birth. Then he made out the necessary report. Mike was later released from the hospital. Unfit for duty, his name was placed on the injured list. In my diary is this note: *He'll be home for Christmas this year!*

The next day, a detective attested to the incident as he applied for an arrest warrant. Because such applications may contain only facts, the detective's report could not include Mike's assumption that Vern did not want Mike to find drugs in the vehicle. Nor could the report refer to Officer Edgar's conjecture that Vern's overheated body suggested he was high on drugs. Other forbidden information was Vern's substantial arrest record: possession of stolen goods, breach of peace, selling a motor vehicle license, selling liquor without a license and the possession of narcotics.

The detective could not mention those things, but he should have included these three omitted facts:

1. The suspect had run three lights, not just two.
2. The man was resisting arrest. Mike reached into the vehicle *after* the party pulled the shifting lever into drive—indicating his intention to flee.

3. Most importantly, Vern had tried to kill Mike. The man had purposely attempted to crush Mike's dangling body between the two cars.

A warrant should have been sought for attempted murder not just assault!

That night, the extremely cold temperature turned out to be a blessing. Mike was wearing his heavy leather police jacket, and it protected his skin as he rolled along the pavement. Another blessing was Officer Edgar's wise decision. He did not squeeze the trigger of his drawn weapon; thus, Mike was saved from further injury. Because Officer Edgar had come around to the driver's side, he did not have a clear shot. A few months earlier, another officer had taken a chance. He had fired off a difficult shot in an attempt to save his partner. His bullet tore into the policeman's back. That officer lost a lung.

Vern was arrested two weeks later for this incident, but it was many months before Mike's assailant was finally in court. Vern gratefully pleaded guilty to a mere Second-Degree Assault charge. He was only sentenced to serve one to four years. (He only served a term of one year and five months.) Mike would be serving a life sentence. He was permanently handicapped.

I served time in personal purgatory. I nursed Mike for many months, and I worried about Vern's release. I confided my concerns only to my diary: *Since Vern's criminal history is one of repetition, I fear he may enter our lives again.*

CHAPTER 5

Choices (1972–1973)

My husband had been more seriously injured on December 9, 1971, than we originally realized. While his abrasions, swollen knee and severe back strain began to heal, his internal bleeding became steadily worse. When he went to the bathroom, there was a red discharge. Because the diarrhea and cramping occurred more and more frequently, our general practitioner referred him to a specialist. The gastroenterologist did a battery of tests and diagnosed ulcerative colitis. He ordered diet therapy and medications. After enduring a strictly liquid diet for two weeks, his condition still had not improved, so he was hospitalized. From April 17, 1972 to May 4, 1972, Mike was not allowed any nourishment by mouth. He was sustained on a liquid prescription, which was ingested by way of a nasal tube. Two months later, Mike returned to work looking like a sumo wrestler. One of his medications (Prednisone) caused a bloating effect, giving him a "moon face".

February 25, 1973: Mike engaged in a fight to subdue an Assault II suspect. During the confrontation, he was accidentally blinded by another officer's mace. The culprit took advantage of the situation and sent a powerful karate kick into Mike's abdomen. Internal bleeding reoccurred. This time treatment included Feosol, Butisol, Prednisone, Paregoric, Cortiform Azulfidine and Imuran. Imuran was a new experimental drug, for which Mike was required to sign papers allowing its use. But this new drug did not stop the internal bleeding. It did, unfortunately, stop hair follicles from growing on his head. It also left unwanted deposits in Mike's eyes. Finally, the conservative specialist had to concede. Since twenty-eight pills per day had not helped, the doctor declared surgery to be the only possible treatment left.

At the surgeon's office, Mike endured a painful sigmoid examination of his mutilated colon. The need for immediate surgery was confirmed. The doctor gave us a shocking description of the radical surgery that he thought necessary. He explained that a total colectomy was the removal of the entire colon (large intestine). Once excised, an abdomino-perineal resection with a permanent ileostomy would be performed. This meant that an abdominal opening would be made, through which the end of his small intestine would be surgically secured. Over it, a disposable pouch would have to be constantly worn.

Mike adamantly refused surgery! He could not accept such a deplorable disability. In denial, he continued hoping that the conservative treatment (complete rest, prescription drugs and a liquid diet) would eventually work. This false hope gave him temporary emotional protection, but very soon, he would be forced to face the terrible reality.

I will never forget those horrid days. We tried to hide the seriousness of Mike's condition from our young children (ages 5 and 7). But they could see his deterioration. My diary relates: *Increased doses of codeine are not effective. It has neither thickened the excrement nor relieved the excruciating pain. He is so thin. He*

*keeps losing more and more weight. Without surgery I fear his death
is imminent.*

I became aware that my children shared this fear when they
began asking significant questions. "When you die, does God
take you away? Where do you go? Why do people have funer-
als? How does your body get out of the ground and go up to
heaven?" Lonny and Lori were frightened by the possibility of
losing their dad. **Death** had introduced itself to them, so I had
to decide how best to control its impact.

How grateful I was to have long ago sought out my own
answers. By delving into books, discussing sermons and wit-
nessing different social rituals, I had developed a healthy attitude about this sensitive subject. I embraced Reverend Tillich's
theory, "If one accepts death, he need not wait for it, with fear
or with contempt." I wanted my children to think of death as
a natural event—one which allows a person to merely pass into
another stage of nature. How could I convince them that *life,
death* and a *thereafter* (whether religious or scientific) was all a
part of eternity. I decided to have a private talk with them the
very next day. While Mike was napping, we sat together on a
couch in the living room. With each beside me, securely cud-
dled in my arms, I began. First, I told them that people had
many different ideas about death. That opened the door for a
lot of questions. I answered as clearly and truthfully as possible.
Lonny questioned, "Why do people have to die?" I tried to convince him of its purpose by explaining, "It allows birth, gives
time meaning and inspires effort." I gave examples, but they
did not fully comprehend. They were just too young. (A book
written by Leo Buscaglia, PhD, would have been a great help.
But *The Fall of Freddie the Leaf* was not published until 1982.)
With frustration, Lori asked, "Why doesn't all that medicine
help?" I honestly admitted that I did not know. In order to end

our discussion on a hopeful note, I told them about the recommended surgery.

Later that night, I found that my assurances had failed. When I went upstairs to check on them, they were huddled together in one bed. Their tear-stained faces indicated that they had quietly cried themselves to sleep. It was a heartbreaking sight. I had to cover my mouth to stifle my own sobbing. I stood there for a long time, despairing at my inability to eliminate their fear. Unable to burden Mike with my discovery, I relieved my beleaguered heart with this diary entry: *How brave they are, trying to keep their secret so they won't add to our worries! I've decided not to say anything. I'll let them believe they succeeded with their act of bravado.* Lonny and Lori never again questioned me about their dad's medical condition, but they did continue to sneak into bed together every night. Their bravery gave me the courage to write this proclamation: *If the worst happens (if Mike dies), we will find a way to survive it. If Mike submits to the debilitating surgery and survives, he will have to find a way to live with it!*

At the end of March, I returned home from lunch duty at my children's school and found Mike collapsed upon the bathroom floor. That was it. I could not watch any more suffering. I would not take part in his agonizing self-destruction. I told him that if he did not agree to the surgery, I would leave him. I shouted the ultimatum, "I'm either calling the hospital, or I am leaving. The choice is yours!"

Mike responded by begrudgingly quoting Pascal's theory, "We live and die alone. No one can help us."

His stubbornness deflated my spirit. My knees buckled, and I went down to the floor next to him. Tears filled my eyes as I quietly assured, "I mean it, Mike. I can't take any more of this. I don't care that you will be handicapped. I want you alive."

Mike raised one hand and gently wiped my escaping tear with his thumb. As he did so, I closed my eyes and nudged my cheek into his caressing palm. I heard him whisper, "All right." It was with great anguish that Mike conceded to the humiliating ileostomy.

I quit my part-time job so that I could give Mike total support. The next week, we revisited the surgeon. Mike brought his police gun belt and asked the doctor to measure his abdomen. The surgeon could only assure that he would try to place the stoma (the opening) low enough to accommodate Mike's wish to once again wear his uniform. If Mike was accepted back on the police force, he would be the only policeman in the United States with such a disability.

Also, during that week, the surgeon arranged for a special visitor. The doctor felt that it would help Mike to better cope with his impending abnormality if he spoke directly with someone who had undergone a similar loss. Knocking at the front door was a recuperated cancer ostomate. *Please let him look healthy and happy* was my quick prayer before turning the doorknob. That prayer was swiftly answered, for on the other side was a healthy male specimen who was only thirty-six years old—just five years older than my husband. Jeff's resolve and candor were encouraging. I excused myself, telling the men that I would make coffee. I knew Mike needed privacy to discuss one very intimate concern. My husband had heard about a catastrophic complication. Surgical nerve damage could cause impotence. Jeff concurred that there was a possibility but quickly added, "The chance for that happening is only 1 percent." In the end, we both benefited from our visitor's expertise. His honest information and sensitive suggestions were very helpful. With relief I wrote: *Mike is a victim, but he now feels less sorry for himself because he has met another person who can truly identify with his own physical and emotional suffering.*

By the end of the week, Mike was admitted to the surgical wing. (Thank God.) He was settled into his hospital bed before being told that his operation was not scheduled for another week! To prevent unexpected complications, he had to be off the experimental medication for one full week before surgery. The time was also needed to build up his strength. Because of Mike's deteriorated condition, he was in need of blood transfusions and hyperalimentation (special intravenous feedings). For this, a shunt had to be sewn into his chest. All this was just preparation for April 18, 1973!

For the next three and one-half weeks, my father and sister volunteered countless hours of babysitting. With their help, I was able to spend twelve hours a day at the hospital, taking an active part in Mike's care. I came home to be with Lonny and Lori for a couple of hours after school. After supper, I returned to the hospital. The surgeon had authorized my unlimited visitation, so I was able to prepare Mike for sleep. I was so busy that only one diary entry was made to describe the whole ordeal: *I'm sure the agony suffered from such a radical surgery can only be comprehended by other ostomates. Fortunately, Mike receives tender loving care from a nurse who herself is an ostomate. She totally understands his needs and is graciously training me so that I may feel comfortable with the necessary medical procedures. This nurse is also sharing her insight about Mike's psychological needs. She warns that Mike's physical healing will be complete long before his psychological healing. Only time will tell how he chooses to deal with it.*

CHAPTER 6

Handicapped but Not Disabled (1973–1974)

Mike would do anything to get out of that hospital room! He convinced his surgeon that I was capable of caring for him. He even agreed to the doctor's conditional mandate: absolute bed rest for another two weeks. His early discharge took place May 4, 1973. The short ride home was exhausting, and Mike's early objections about going straight to bed were immediately forgotten.

Three more long months of recuperation followed. Finally, August arrived, and the surgeon reluctantly signed a "return to work" slip. Because Mike anticipated a problem at the police department, he also garnered written permission from his gastroenterologist. Armed with two verifications, he reported to the watch commander. Mike was shocked by his crass opinion, "They're not going to let you back with a 'shit bag'. I was told they're putting you on disability."

Mike immediately asked to see the chief. The chief was not in, so Mike was directed to the deputy chief, a man for whom Mike had great respect. He was the same captain to whom I had given periodic updates about Mike's condition. During those conversations, I not only described Mike's physical ordeal, but openly divulged his psychological struggle as well. My husband was having difficulty accepting his demeaning handicap, so I needed to explain just how important it was for Mike to return to his job as a police officer. Mike regarded it as a job for a **real man**—a whole man. My diary affirms the compassionate help given by the deputy chief: *Bless his heart. He accepted the responsibility of assigning Mike to light-duty in the Evidentiary Service Division. His only stipulation was that Mike also get a medical release from the city's doctor.*

Mike showed the city "doc" the opinions of his other two doctors, then produced the assignment order for light duty. As the doctor was reviewing the medical reports, Mike quietly declared, "I deserve the chance to try." The doctor capitulated but made it very clear that Mike's return was on a trial basis only.

August 13, 1973, diary entry: *I watched out the kitchen window today as Mike walked to his metallic beige Nova parked in the driveway. The unbidden visage of his once large sumo physique instantly came to mind. On his last day of work, Mike had that drug produced swollen look with a 'moon-face'. What a contrast to the wiry stick of a man now raising his second spit-shined shoe into the car! Sensing me watching, he turned his head and gave me a broad, encouraged smile, then waved good-bye. I will never be more proud of him than I was at that moment! Handicapped with an ileostomy, but endowed with determination, Mike went in pursuit of his police career. God speed.*

Light duty continued. Mike was sent to fingerprint school and spent six months comparing and classifying prints. While I was enjoying this safe office assignment, Mike was becoming very restless. He missed being a street cop. Finally, when he could stand it no longer, he went to see the deputy chief.

Once again, the captain understood. He knew how much Mike needed regular duty, and he believed that Mike could handle it. He granted Mike's request. On February 4, 1974, Mike returned to the Field Service Division as a uniformed patrolman—**handicapped but able!**

CHAPTER 7

Nurse or Mom (1973)

During Mike's lengthy recuperation, I was worried that I may have to become our family's breadwinner, so I had enrolled in an LPN (Licensed Practical Nurse) school. The nursing course was only twelve straight months, which meant that much of it would be behind me by the time my husband's healing was complete. I loved it! With Mike home watching over the house and children, I was able to maintain above-average grades, placing second in the class.

Mike was allowed to return to work! Unfortunately, he came home exhausted and was unable to help as much as he once did. For me, finding time to study became harder and harder. Then Mike was rotated to B-Squad (4:00 PM to 12:00 AM). This shift left me solely responsible for the children's after-school and evening care. Often, they would arrive home a half hour before me. This always left in question just who the daily survivor would be. After peace treaties were negotiated between siblings, dinner had to be made. Lonny needed to be transported to hockey practice twice a week. Lori had dance class once a week, and both brought home schoolwork that deserved review. My nursing shoes had to be polished, and everyone's clothes had to be ironed for wearing the next day. It was often eleven o'clock by the time my family chores were complete. Then I could study. I greeted Mike when he got home, but he often went to bed without me. I worked until 1:30 AM or 2:00 AM. My alarm went off at 5:45 AM so that I could report for the 7:00 AM to 3:00 PM shift at the hospital! At least Mike was able to cover the morning shift at home. He got the children off to school. With this schedule, my grade point average dropped to 85 percent, but I was determined to endure.

My son, Lonny, taxed that resolve. He became ill. Skin test showed several allergies, and blood tests showed three different viruses. (Many people prone to allergies also have immune deficiencies.) But what could not be shown with medical testing was the cause of his psychosomatic problem—I called it "schoolitis".

An allergist recommended environmental controls within the home and administered weekly injections. Time was the only thing that could relieve his viral symptoms, and Mom had to be responsible for the rest. My expertise was needed to relieve Lonny's stress and make him feel that, for a change, **he** was my top priority! So with just three months left to complete the nursing course, I allowed my love for my son to outweigh my desire to become a nurse. It was with deep regret that I wrote my withdrawal letter.

My thought: *I am afraid this goal will never be reached, but my recompense will be a happy child. Besides, knowledge is never a waste. With Mike's job, my medical training will be very useful.*

CHAPTER 8

A Big Brass Band (1974)

Independence Day, 8:30 AM. I had already fed Lonny and Lori breakfast, and my husband's scrambled eggs and cheese mixture was sitting in a bowl, ready to be poured into a skillet. Lonny had already stored the lawn chairs in the trunk of the car, while Lori had fed and watered the dog. Both children had even made their beds without complaint! They were now anxious to wake their father. If they did not arrive early, they would not get to sit on the corner where the parade turned onto Main Street!

Because their dad had not gotten into bed until 3:30 AM, I decided it would be best if I were the one to wake him. I was sure that the children's method would arouse a grump. Even though I felt like a villainess, I gently nudged him. Since Mike had promised to partake in this family outing, I continued my impudence. I was going to make sure that the children were not disappointed. Finally, Mike moaned his annoyance, "What time is it?"

"Eight thirty."

"Jesus!" he lamented.

I quietly reminded, "Mike, you have to get up. You promised to take the kids to see the parade."

Actually, I was in need of his attention just as much as the children. I needed to feel like a protected wife with an attentive husband who was willing to share a special day. I wanted to walk hand in hand together across the grass as we followed after our excited children.

"Can't you take the kids?" Mike cajoled.

My answer was unequivocal. "No I can't!" The idea was repugnant. Too often Mike's crazy work schedule made Lonny, Lori and I a threesome. He missed softball games, baseball games, hockey games, dance recitals and open house. Today, police work was no excuse because this holiday happened to fall on Mike's scheduled day off. I was therefore relentless. I released both room-darkening shades with a sharp snap and pulled the sheet from him. Still in a daze, Mike squinted his blurry eyes and raised his forearm as a shield against the glaring sun. He gazed upon the silhouette at the foot of his bed. There I stood with feet spread apart and hands on both hips, affecting a no-nonsense stance. As his eyes adjusted to the brightness, my features came into focus, and he could see that the reproof in my eyes was mingled with hurt. That revelation deflated his intended diatribe, and contrition forced his feet over the side of the bed. Guilt would not allow him to be a naysayer. The children, who were not privy to Mom's silent coercion, came bounding upon the bed. With bright smiles, they informed their dad that they had been patiently waiting since 7:00 AM! Their bubbling enthusiasm encouraged him to hurry.

The town went all-out every year! Clowns, high school and military bands, drum and bugle corps, Shriners' mini cars, balloons, fire trucks, scouts and horses all vied for the attention of the happy onlookers. Adults raised themselves out of folding chairs and off of street curbs whenever an American flag passed by. Their display of respect encouraged children to follow their fine example. Appreciation was made openly apparent as the audience applauded each group parading by. Everybody was on their best behavior, displaying good manners and thoughtfulness toward strangers sitting next to them. Everyone was having a wonderful time!

After the last group passed, our family meandered the path leading back to our parked car. While the children were in a deep discussion trying to decide which band had been the best, Mike placed his arm around my shoulders, gave me a gentle hug, and said, "Thank you."

"For what?" I smiled.

Without hesitation, he replied, "For today. I almost forgot that there are still a lot of nice people in the world. I only get to see the bad."

I encircled his waist with my right arm, and we continued walking in harmonious silence. (It was an acquired habit to walk on Mike's left, the opposite side from where he wore his off-duty gun concealed high upon his hip.) While Mike was taking breaths of newborn optimism, I was thinking about the indoctrination meeting I had attended with other police wives four years before. I recalled the speaker's proclamation, "You, police wives, have an awesome responsibility. Each of you must keep your husband's feet on the ground and his head on straight." Now, I fully understood what he had meant. Circumstances in law enforcement nurture cynicism, suspicion and pessimism. The officer's wife must keep these negative attitudes at bay.

CHAPTER 9

Making a Difference (1974)

My daughter's earlier abstract concept of death became a vivid reality on May 4, 1974. I was driving my father's car. He was in the passenger seat, and Lori was in the back seat. Suddenly, Dad placed his hand to his head.

Even though my father was unconscious, I tried to remain calm for Lori's sake. I told her that I would need her help to get Grandfather to the hospital. From the back seat, she stood, valiantly supporting his head so that he would not fall toward me as we sped to the nearest hospital. Along the way, I flagged down a police cruiser. The officers appraised the situation and agreed there was no time to wait for an ambulance. I slid over into the middle seat so that one patrolman could take over the driving. The other officer returned to his cruiser to provide an escort. During the short trip, I reassured my father that we would soon be at the hospital. I stopped speaking only when I felt his body relax and heard his last soft exhale. When the shrilling siren stopped outside the emergency room, I knew we were too late.

My beloved father was dead on arrival, but I could not yet tell Lori. Instead, I instructed her to stay in the waiting room while I followed the gurney into a cubicle. I had to make sure that Dad's wishes were fulfilled. The doctor was not to call a "code blue". (During past conversations, my father had made it very clear that he would rather die than survive the next stroke as a vegetable.) The attending physician dictated the time of death.

Once I collected myself, I reluctantly went out to the waiting room to give Lori the devastating news. She made me so proud! There were tears but no hysteria. Shortly she managed a small smile and uttered this profound comment, "Grandfather got his wish."

Because of ill health, my father had openly discussed his pending death with the entire family. His frank talks and his peaceful death rendered solace to a child who had become overly concerned about the "endless fires of purgatory". Lori's Catholic friend had been preparing for her first communion, and her preaching had literally frightened Lori into nightmares. After viewing her grandfather's quiet passing, the nightmares stopped.

My fear that Lori was going to be traumatized by this experience was unfounded. Instead, she learned a valuable lesson: If you don't fear death, you can enjoy life. Thank you, Dad.

Lori later referred to other teachings from her grandfather. The following is a college English paper:

An Unusual Learning Place

> *From 1966 to 1974 much of my education took place in a small, four-door classroom with beige interior, many glass windows, wall-to-wall carpeting and two bench seats. This 1965 Dodge Dart provided me with many experiences from infancy into my seventh year. Any*

trip, short or long, was a lesson. Grandfather used this time to teach me many things: math, reading, music, courtesy and safety.

I learned math by counting trucks and watching the speedometer and odometer. The distance between places always did fascinate me. His teachings eliminated the question, "Are we there yet?" Letters were learned from street signs and advertisements painted on buses and bill-boards. We enjoyed music, both sing-a-longs and the AM radio. I learned that courtesy and safety are very important as Grandfather allowed pedestrians to cross and graciously gave others the right-of-way. Trash was never thrown out of his windows, and hands and heads were (for the most part) kept inside. I learned responsibility through hours of washing, rinsing and waxing; I learned that things could last a long time if well-cared for. His 1965 Dart was still in good shape on May 4, 1974 when he died in it!

Even in death he remained a teacher. I was a passenger on that day. My mother and I had driven his Dart to the bus terminal to pick him up. (He had given up driving for fear of hurting others should he have another stroke or heart attack while at the wheel of his car.) We had driven only a few blocks from the bus terminal when his hand went to his head and he slumped backward. His two previous heart attacks and one stroke had convinced my grandfather to wish for a sudden death. He had no fear. His

49

*calm acceptance of the inevitable taught **me** not to fear death.*

I still remember every lesson taught in his little Dodge Dart.

CHAPTER 10

Lawsuits (1974–1975)

Section 31-293 of the Worker's Compensation Act declares: If the injured employee brings action against a third person, the employer may join as a party plaintiff. After the deduction of expenditures for recovery (court and lawyer), rewarded damages shall be proportioned so that **the claim of the employer shall take precedence over that of the injured employee.** The employer's claim consists of 1.) the amount of compensation paid (incapacity payment, surgical, medical and hospital services); 2.) an amount equal to any probable future payments. Mike's future compensation payments would last a lifetime. Pouches, powder, belts, solvent and special tape are recorded monthly. Medication is needed to prevent excessive flow, which could cause dehydration. One complication had already caused excruciating pain, which sent Mike to the emergency room. Scar tissue had caused an obstruction, and he had to be admitted.

Grateful that his compensation carrier continued to take care of all his medical needs, Mike willingly agreed to the insurance company's request to sue for **their** reimbursement. A January 3, 1974 newspaper article read: "A policeman has filed a $50,000 damage suit in Superior Court against a motor-

ist who allegedly dragged the officer 50-feet along Allen Ave."
Since the *convicted* assailant owned and operated an automotive
repair shop, readers must have thought Mike was going to experience a windfall!

Mike would not receive any of this money. In fact, he had
to use his own personal car insurance policy. He had $2,500
coverage for an uninsured motorist (which Vern was). Because
of the Workers' Compensation Act, this money had to be turned
over to the employer's compensation carrier for reimbursement.
On March 27, 1974, Mike signed over the following money:

$143.90—Court Cost.

$833.33—Lawyer Fee (necessary to assure
Mike's proper compensation).

$1,522.77—Employer
Compensation Reimbursement.

Mike's responsibility was fulfilled. Vern's accountability
was another matter!

The lawsuit against Mike's assailant was useless. A damage settlement could not be imposed upon Vern! The repair/
used-car business was exempt because it constituted his livelihood. (No one had yet proven that Vern used the establishment
for dealing drugs and fencing cars). His home was safeguarded
because the mortgage was in his mother's name. Thus, it was
determined that he was without obtainable assets.

Should Vern ever acquire any unprotected assets in the
future, Mike's lawyer took steps for possible damage reimbursement at that time. In June 1975, Mike's attorney also arranged
for Vern's license, then under suspension, to remain so until

Mike's claim was satisfied. The Motor Vehicle Department would restrict Vern until they received a satisfaction notice from Mike's attorney. Mike's opinion about these new tactics was one of resignation. "This only serves as a mere irritant to Vern. He is smart enough to hide his assets, and now that he is out of jail, I'm told he just drives around without a license."

By December 1975, the Compensation Commission had completed paying for 121.04 weeks of incapacity wages, totaling $11,500. From it, Mike's lawyer took his $2,875 for fees. Mike was left with $8,625. Because Mike only displayed strength, most people believed he was fully recovered. Only I understood his ongoing psychological battle. My diary confirms: *He still has trouble dealing with the fact that he must live with a mutilated body. He so hates his abnormality that few people know of his handicap. Even though I respect his wishes for secrecy, my feelings are quite the opposite. I've told him, 'Instead of being embarrassed, you should be proud. You don't let it stop you from doing anything.' I've tried to convince him that self is not lost with a body part but in one's mind.*

CHAPTER 11

Collisions (1974)

May 1974: Mike was a passenger during a high-speed chase that ended with a head-on collision. After the apprehension, Mike went to the ER. He called me with his own diagnosis: "I'm a little banged up." The doctor ordered rest, hot packs and physical therapy for his neck and back.

November 1974: Mike was once again a passenger in a black-and-white. They were responding to a burglar alarm when a driver failed to yield for their siren. The cruiser was T-boned on Mike's side. The ER diagnosis: concussion, right ankle sprain, and neck pain.

CHAPTER 12

Trauma (1975)

At age eleven, Lonny had his own experience with death. The incident had been so traumatic that he could still vividly recall it for an English paper seven years later. Lonny remembered how impatiently he had awaited that particular morning because the day's plans had promised excitement! He wrote:

More than a Fishing Trip

I awoke very early. The frigid temperature convinced me to take out my heaviest pair of jeans, a winter jacket and boots; my mother also insisted I wear long-johns and a knit hat! Without quibbling, I happily prepared for this special day. I had been invited to go along with the grown-ups, my father and two fellow police officers. We were going fishing for bass!

As we started off, I had great expectations. My excitement only grew as Dad and I drove to the river to meet his friends. I couldn't wait to get out in the boat and drop my line into the water! My patience was tested when Pete had difficulty starting the boat's stubborn engine; I couldn't help thinking that I'd be catching no fish today. It seemed our long-planned fishing trip was going to be over even before it had begun. Suddenly, my pout was replaced with a childish grin. We finally got under way.

It was a thrilling feeling to rush away from the shore. As the distance grew, cold feet suddenly caught my attention. From somewhere up front, the boat had sprung a very fast leak. My heart started to pound. I didn't know what to do. The beach was getting farther and farther away, and the water was inching up my boots! My frenzied mind told me, "If I wait any longer, I won't be able to make it to shore." With no further thought, I jumped alone into the river and began to struggle against the swift current. It was a long swim for anyone, but for a boy with boots and a winter jacket, it was impossible.

About twenty yards from the bank, my forward progress stopped! All my strength was engaged in the fight to stay surfaced. It seemed as if my mind had become separated from my body because I could see my arms beating wildly, but I could not feel them. I didn't realize that these were symptoms of hypothermia. My mind only comprehended that the embankment was not getting any closer—I wasn't going to make it. I was going to die! I began to sink. But at that very moment a strong hand pushed me upward. It was my father! His determination and strength saved us both!

For quite some time we lay shivering on the muddy bank catching our breath. Only my eyes had the strength to move, and they followed my new tackle box which easily stayed afloat! It bobbed along riding the current down river. Somehow, its loss did not seem very important.

Once everyone was safe, my Dad and I mustered the strength to make our way to the car with its welcomed heater. As we thawed, we began to laugh about the terrifying experience. On the way home we joked about the loss of a brand new fishing pole and the fish it might inadvertently catch at the bottom. Chip's dedication to saving the yet unopened six-pack of Budweiser brought more harmonious laughter. The camaraderie temporarily relieved our tension, but eventually silence prevailed as we both thought about **what could have happened!** *Dad had promised me a special day; it certainly was—even without my bass!*

Upon their arrival home, I viewed their soggy clothes and chattering teeth with alarm, but it was not until bedtime that Mike and I could openly talk. Learning all the details was even more alarming! Lonny had not been wearing a life jacket because it did not fit over his winter coat. Even more sobering was Mike's disclosure that he, who could swim like a fish, had doubts about ever getting out of the freezing water.

My diary confides: *A shiver runs down my spine thinking about it, but there is a positive outcome to this near tragedy.*

Lonny will never again doubt his father's love, which has, at times, been in question when Mike misses his school and sports activities. Learning that his dad would have died with him rather than leave him was a wonderful discovery. It has assured Lonny that his dad will always be there for him—whatever, whenever and wherever his need. Unfortunately, there is a downside as well. Lonny may be tortured by fearful dreams for some time to come.

CHAPTER 13

Equal Rights (1975)

Winter, 1975: City officials decided to introduce "City Residency Requirements" upon their police officers. They theorized that such a mandate would create the following:

1. Increased Revenue: Payroll expenditures will be returned to the coffer as officers spend their salaries within the city. This is essential during this time of economic instability.
2. More Protection: Police numbers will triple because both off-duty squads will be in the city, and every officer will be expected to respond to any criminal incidents witnessed. Emergency response time will be minimized in times of crisis.
3. Greater Community Awareness: Residency will stimulate personal involvement.

While seeking such admirable goals, the administration neglected a most significant aspect. They perceived the affected personnel only as cops and not human beings (men and women, husbands and wives, fathers and mothers). They totally disregarded the fact that these are people with citizens' rights. Mike and I felt their theory was flawed because confining officers (giving them no right to choose where to live) makes them second-class citizens. Other city employees had no such restriction. Business personnel and hospital staff had no such restriction. My diary entry shows just how adamant I felt: *Advertisements for police department employment should read: Jobs Available: Second-class citizens needed to protect first-class citizens.*

Mike and I believed that the mandate would not produce the expected beneficial goals but would instead produce unexpected detrimental consequences. We knew that many police families would refuse to leave their established suburban homes where they felt safe. These experienced police officers would be seeking unrestricted employment elsewhere. A few officers would relocate but would do so begrudgingly. Some would merely establish a false residence. The residency issue may prove to be the "last straw" and cause a few divorces. Any of these scenarios would adversely affect the quality of law enforcement in the city.

Mike knew that constant attrition required periodic hiring, and finding intelligent, psychologically-sound people who were willing to take such a job was already an ongoing problem. Since the city's reservoir could only supply so many suitable people, such restrictions would sorely hamper quality hiring. He questioned, "Why would high-caliber outsiders be interested in this restrictive city when other cities offered them employment without residency requirements?"

Officers should not be cops twenty-four hours a day. Since this extremely important fact was also overlooked, I made an effort to enlighten city administrators and the general public. I submitted my thoughts to every city councilman and to the city newspaper. To my surprise, the local newspaper published my anonymous letter on the editorial page. Beneath it was this statement: "In this rare exception to our rule against printing unsigned letters, the paper has satisfied itself as to the author's identity." (Not true.)

*I wish to offer my thoughts about this controversial police housing situation. My husband has been a devoted officer in your city for five years. It is his belief that **not** being a resident offers benefits to both himself and to the public which he serves. For him, living in a suburban home allows vital separation from his taxing work. Police psychologists agree that periodic detachment is a healthy and necessary safeguard for an officer's personality, objectivity and usefulness. Being able to leave the city at the end of his shift allows the officer to totally disassociate himself from the burdens of rape, murder, robberies, assaults, illness and death. It allows him time to become refreshed and renewed before his next exposure. The public benefits as the officer is then more able to be cool and objective. His family also benefits because distance from the cop's world allows him to more easily enter their world where he can concentrate on being a husband, father, brother or son. In this private world, interaction with family and friends rejuvenates his faith in mankind. Neighbors do not look upon the officer as the next-door cop from whom favors are expected, and the entire family is more readily accepted as friends. This world*

also allows the family more safety from harass-
ment, obscene phone calls and vengeful lunatics.

I hope that you will continue to extend
to your police officers the same equal rights
extended by your city to their other employees,
by all businesses to their men and women and
by both hospitals to their doctors and nurses.

Allow the police officer a life of his own. He
needs off-duty time, time when he can remove
his gun and become just another man.

A Policeman's Wife

The city tried to continue its implementation of this mandate, but so many officers refused to comply that an extension was issued. I made this diary entry: *Many officers continue to hope that any town within a ten-mile radius will be acceptable. Even those living further away have hopes of being granted "Grandfather Immunity". Right now, only new cadets are being forced into city residency. The police union is bringing a class action suit against the city on their behalf. I am still in fear of losing my home or separating from my husband. Mostly, I fear making the choice! How can I bring my children into such a city?*

Mike also had an article in the newspaper. Mike was pictured leaning against his cruiser's open door. The photo was taken from the front so that the massive damage to his black-and-white could be seen. The driver of a stolen vehicle had lost control during a high-speed chase. The thief's car spun out when he tried to turn a corner. The spinning ended when it collided with the front end of Mike's cruiser. Mike suffered a painful back sprain.

CHAPTER 14

Compassion-Passion (1975)

Compassion. Mike was responding to a sick call in a housing project when he was forced to stop his cruiser. A young man had stepped out in front of him. The youth was obeying a rule of this jungle: detain any officer at any time whenever possible. Mike told the boy, "I don't have time for this nonsense. Someone is ill and needs help." The boy slowly moved on. Mike proceeded to a home where a woman was lying unconscious on the kitchen floor. Mike began to administer oxygen while awaiting an ambulance. Suddenly, the woman's son came bursting through the door. It was the same teenager who had detained him earlier.

As Mike was telling me about this, I interrupted, "I hope you told his father that you could have been there sooner if not for his son's interference."

Mike responded, "I didn't say a word. I didn't have to. You should have seen the look on that kid's face."

At another time, Mike was called to a bank to effect the arrest of a sixteen-year-old girl who was caught trying to pass a bad check. It seemed prostitution was off that day, and she badly needed a fix. While awaiting the transport wagon, Mike bought her a Coke in hope that it may help. Unfortunately, her hands were shaking so badly that she spilled most of the soda all over his pants. That night when Mike told me about the incident, he was truly saddened. This beautiful young girl's life had been ruined by drugs.

Passion. "There is always time for loving," Mike declared as he reached out from the couch to catch my wrist.

I half-heartedly denied, "I can't. My bus is due at the high school in half an hour." But Mike slowly pulled me down on top of him. (Why do we have to live by the clock?)

"No one is going anywhere without you." The words tickled my ear as he began to ever so gently kiss my neck. Methodically his lips traveled to every part of my face.

My reserve melted. Mike had again succeeded in manipulating me to the point of desire, and I sought his mouth. I was unaware that Mike had slid us down to the carpet. I was only aware of the familiar longing as our lips became urgent.

CHAPTER 15

Sacrifices (1976)

Several months went by, and the city's residency mandate was still looming over our heads. We were advised to send a personal letter of appeal to the city manager.

Dear Sir,

I am the wife of a police officer who has for six years devoted himself to your city. In those years, he has always done his utmost to uphold the laws which assure those moral rights which are yours.

He has, in fact, given far too much of himself. On several occasions, his own physical well-being has been jeopardized. The most serious injury occurring in 1971 left him with a permanent ileostomy. It took months of fortitude to regain his strength and return to active street duty. How much more must he sacrifice?

His family has made their fair share of sacrifices too. During those stressful months when his father was seriously ill, Lonny (our young son) began daily vomiting, experienced severe headaches and became indifferent to his school work. These psychosomatic symptoms fell short of causing a stomach ulcer but did cause the loss of a full year of scholastic achievement.

Due to the difficult working hours inherent in the police profession, our daughter, Lori, has missed the joy of her father's approval when she slugs that big white softball. She has missed his company at her school's Open House and at her choir's performance downtown.

I have spent many sleepless nights waiting for the sound of his footsteps when he'd had to work late. I've also spent many hours nursing him back to health, knowing, full well that there will be a next time. Holidays are continually a disappointment. New Year's Eve is traditionally a night for me to curl up alone in front of the TV. For you to now dictate that we must sacrifice our home is beyond belief!

My husband, Mike, and I have worked for twelve years to turn a run-down, starter house into a warm, attractive home for our children who have never known another. Every extra cent has been put into remodeling, redecorating, making additions and general upkeep. Our children help with the yard work; to all of us, our miniature castle is priceless.

The police chief's letter informed us that exceptions may be granted in cases of extreme *hardship. Besides the insecurity and emotional stress upon all, other hardships would be:*

1. *The loss of a convenient free ostomy clinic for my husband.*

2. *The loss of educational opportunities. My husband would not be able to graduate from the community college he is now attending for an Associate Degree in criminology.*

Lori now has the opportunity to attend school where a unique level placement program enables her to accelerate above normal. My son has the option of an exceptional trade school, should he so choose that route. (At that time, we never dreamed he'd obtain a Master's Degree!)

3. *The loss of financial security. A new mortgage with today's incredible interest rates would be disastrous. Rather than commute, I would have to give up my meager job in search for another, and my children would lose the $15 per week they earn from their paper route.*

4. *The loss of personal self-worth. Are your police officers merely tin soldiers to be toyed with? Can't you care about them as human beings, husbands and fathers?*

Since the chief has already verified that our present residence has in no way adversely affected the performance of my husband's duty, I can honestly request your sincere consider-

ation. Please do not force us into a move which would tear up our family's roots, jeopardize our financial security and cause my children much unhappiness.

With hopes that you will allow us to stay in our home, I remain:

A Distraught Wife

I feared my appeal would be read by a shortsighted politician, but I was pleasantly surprised. We were allowed to remain in our home. In fact, we are still living in our "little castle" at the top of the hill.

CHAPTER 16

More Injuries (1975–1976)

On January 9, 1975, Mike's neck was still bothering him. A test revealed that his neck had a foraminal encroachment on the right C5-6 and cervical lordosis at the C6-7. Treatment: medication and rest.

October 1975: While driving in a high-speed chase, Mike's right ankle snapped when he was hard-breaking into a turn. ER diagnosis: ligament strain and bone chips. Treatment: medication for swelling and pain, ice pack, ace bandage and crutches.

July 1976: Mike slipped off a curb and reinjured his right ankle while assisting another officer to make an arrest. Surgical intervention was now needed. On August 27, 1976, a ligament transfer was done. The orthopedic surgeon drilled a hole through the ankle bone and thread the torn ligament through the opening before reattaching it. This Evan's Procedure was supposed to support the ligament. Mike returned to work in December (five months later).

CHAPTER 17

College Bound (1974–1977)

During these years a city police officer, who wished to better himself, could attend college on a free scholarship provided by the government. Mike and a good friend entered a nearby community college. The department accommodated their college schedule by exempting them from the mandated cycle of days off and monthly shift changes. Mike's off-duty injury time gave him more time to study. Since Mike and his friend could have the same two days off every week, they arranged to take classes together. Of course, they took all the interesting police courses first, leaving English classes to the very last. At the time, Mike was unaware of the significance of developing his writing skills. He did not know that his future would include twelve years of detective work, which would require thousands of hours for factual reports and articulate testimony. Mike's first English assignment was to write about a hero:

My Son, My Son

> *Lonny, after more than twenty hours of struggle, pushed his nine-pound, two-ounce*

*body into the world on September 21, 1964.
After this major victory, I suppose the battles
to come were trivial. The first of Lonny's skirmishes was with a new nourishment called formula. Even though his mouth abided its taste,
his stomach often rejected it! He often suffered
in terrible pain which could only be relieved
by a long, back-thumping ride upon a shoulder. Then came skimmed milk and a new challenge—food. Some baby food tasted so horrible,
he couldn't help sneezing or coughing to evict
the strange matter from his mouth. It took all
of his restraint and fortitude to survive while a
compromising menu was established.*

*Other altercations ensued when he began
to receive toys. They were often more frustrating
than fascinating. So, the war began. First with
a defense which consisted of chewing, throwing
and crying. Then the offense began—studying,
pushing and pulling. Lonny's persistence made
him "Conqueror of All Toys".*

*The most perplexing enemies were his own
two awkward extremities—legs. When the right
flank advanced, the left flank would retreat,
leaving Lonny in a precarious position. Again,
however, he succeeded. His endurance and courage prevailed.*

*"Stand up." "Don't touch." "Sit." "Eat it."
"Spit it out." These commands were quickly
comprehended, but how to communicate a reply
was a problem. Lonny's strategy was once again
defense with the word "NO." Then the offense*

began with "Ma-ma", "Da-da" and "pause"
(meaning please).

By the age of one year, my son having
endured through numerous encounters, emerged
the victor. I, his proud father, remain astonished
by my son, my hero.

Mike's English paper was returned with a B- grade and a note from the professor: "Effective—good quality—topic sustained, but not enough material." I disagreed with the professor's evaluation as so noted in my diary entry: *This work deserves an A+ because the author is a cop who has been able to relinquish his tough-guy persona and expose a caring human being.*

After three years, Mike receive his Associate's Degree for criminology. In June 1977, he graduated with a 3.52 grade point average.

CHAPTER 18

Mother Nature's Assault (1977)

The winter of 1977 brought a terrible ice storm that shut down New England. All police officers worked extended shifts to cover related emergencies. After twelve hours of sliding around in his police cruiser, Mike was finally able to scrape off his old VW. (I used the new car.) He anticipated only one more hour of slipping and sliding before he could collapse into his warm bed. He would indeed find himself in bed. Unfortunately, it was not his own!

The highway into suburbia was deserted, but several miles out, Mike did approach a determined tractor-trailer truck. Since road conditions did not allow passing, Mike was still following behind it when thick ice suddenly peeled away from the top of the trailer. He tried to swerve in order to avoid the enormous flying chunk. There was not enough time. Its impact against the windshield caused Mike to react spontaneously. He hit the brakes. This caused him to lose control, and the car went into a spin. As it slammed into a large ice-glazed snowbank, Mike was thrown from the car. His body was hurled over the roadside's embankment. There he lay unconscious. A patrolling state trooper found him sometime later.

Frozen blood was crusted across Mike's right temple, and it also frosted the once white snow. The state trooper notified the city and asked them to call Mike's family. Since he was unconscious, someone would have to give medical consent. The city sent one of their officers to pick me up. By the time we arrived, an hour and thirty minutes had gone by since my phone call to ER personnel. I hurried into the treatment area—looking into every cubicle as I rushed past. At first, I went right by Mike. His face and head were so swollen that I had not recognized him. What a horrific sight! Many stitches closed a large laceration which stretched from Mike's eyebrow into his hairline.

"Mike?" I quietly questioned.

He opened his eyes and squinted. "Hi."

Thank God.

The doctor told me that Mike had a severe concussion and should be admitted, but there was no available bed. The hospital was at full capacity due to the storm. Since no ambulance driver was willing to drive "unnecessarily" on such dangerous roads, Officer Paul and I had to transport him ourselves. It was a slow trip to the hospital close to our home. Mike would spend five days in a darkened hospital room.

I wrote the following poem about this incident:

Recollections

There lay his body on top of the pristine white snow.
He'd been unconscious. How long? He didn't know!
His last memory was of the car radio,
Playing his favorite music, just a bit low.

Suddenly, he had visions of bright hospital lights.
Their shapes were distorted; nothing was quite
right.
As the doctor was checking his blurry eyesight,
The nurse applied pressure upon the bleeding
site.

His head felt as if it were severed down to his
brain.
The swelling became profuse as he lay there in
pain.
Weight from the ice pack he so utterly disdained,
That spontaneous cursing could not be refrained.

After many x-rays and much consultation,
It was decided there'd be no operation.
An intern was ordered, "Sew the laceration."
Then, "Doc" Brown went to his next
examination.

"No beds available," claimed the administration.
So, stitched like a zipper and on pain medication,
We drove miles, worrying about complications;
More nausea, vomiting, or hallucinations.

Near home, we called his own doctor to see,
If he'd appraise the situation more carefully.
"I've arranged your hospital admittance," said
he.
"You need total rest, observation and IVs."

If Mike would give them his full cooperation,

There would be one week of hospitalization,
Followed by two weeks "at home" recuperation.
Severe headaches would make it no vacation!

His lieutenant was assured that he'd return soon,
Capable and ready to once again resume,
*Dealing with **ordinary** dangers that always loom;*
Tempers that easily fume; guns that go boom-boom.

For many weeks after this terrible ordeal,
His nightmares recreated the brakes that did squeal,
As he swerved to avoid the ice chunk which had peeled
From the top of the trailer, behind which he'd wheeled.

Although more police injuries are expected,
Michael's fear of their happening is rejected.
Thus, he returns with memories recollected.
Of that winter night when he was resurrected.

Me, I cope by keeping busy with diversions.
Writing diary notes relieves much tension.
It helps keep my fear in proper dimension.
*Worry **will not** become an obsession!*

CHAPTER 19

Mob Mentality (1977)

It was 9:15 PM on a warm summer's evening when the dispatcher called out for any line unit who could assist Unit 55. That officer had responded to an active fight complaint, which involved a weapon, and he was alone in the "Square" (a huge low-income housing project) where a large crowd was gathering. Mike was the first backup to arrive. As of yet, the group was merely boisterous.

Mike purposely left his police hat in his cruiser. He wanted to weave his way through the horde as unobtrusively as possible in order to reach the lone patrolman and the victim who were at its core. Mike successfully traversed the masses and gained access to the casualty, a teenage Puerto Rican boy who declared that he had been struck in the back with a baseball bat. He pointed out his assailant, a black woman still present among the crowd. Two other officers made their way into the center of the group just as the victim was telling Mike that he wanted his attacker arrested. Mike then tried to approach the alleged assailant, but several people stepped in front of her to make a human shield. Because each was yelling their own rendition of the incident, several minutes passed before Mike could confront the accused female, whose identity was still unknown. Her input had been concise. "Go fuck yourself! You're not going to arrest me!" At that point, he did inform her that she was under arrest, but she immediately took flight with the aid of people who grabbed Mike. More people abetted by encircling the other officers as well. After a short verbal confrontation, the policemen were allowed their freedom. EMTs arrived to transport the boy to the hospital as the officers took foot pursuit, **walking** in the direction taken by the fleeing suspect. Mike used his portable radio to give out their direction of travel and a description of the female suspect.

About seventy-five yards across the courtyard, they encountered further interference. A juvenile's fist struck Mike in the back. As he turned, she spat into his face. She then adamantly protested, "You're not going to arrest my sister!" Mike looked over her head and quickly surveyed their following audience. The rowdy mob had grown enormously and was now approximately 200 in number! Their presence called for rational thought, so he quelled his anger enough to use some common sense. Subduing this young female in front of these people would only incite more parties into violence. He could take her into custody later. Right now, he had to force himself to walk away. But she was persistent! She pursued Mike, pummeling him with her fists. Her wild assault excited the other onlookers into action. They began to throw rocks and bottles at all three policemen. To no avail, the housing project's brave security guards tried to dissuade those people whom they knew. During the fracas, Mike barely heard the sergeant's radio transmission telling them he was driving down the street. Very soon, his cruiser would be at their location. Hearing this, the patrolmen subdued the thirteen-year-old and made a dash for the sergeant's approaching vehicle. All the while, projectiles continued to assail them. Once inside the vehicle, their sergeant threw his cruiser into reverse and sped backward down the street. He then performed a perfect 180-degree turn and quickly drove his officers to their unattended cruisers. These parked units had to be rescued from the impending damage, which they would surely sustain. By 9:45 PM, the "young lady" was being transported to the juvenile authorities, and the officers were tending to their contusions and abrasions. ER x-rays were taken of Mike's bruised right wrist and left elbow. A flying brick had caused both tendon damage and a bone chip in his elbow.

What a night! The Puerto Rican male victim was only fourteen. The black girl that was arrested was only thirteen. The female batter was still at large. And who knew what further violence would follow because of this racial incident!

It made me think about my own children. I wrote in my diary: *I fear for my children who are now eleven and thirteen, for they must not assimilate into such a society.*

CHAPTER 20

A Disastrous Autumn (1978)

September 1978: Mike sustained a broken right upper molar and neck pain. His cruiser had bottomed out while driving at a high speed to reach an officer calling for help.

October 1978: Mike's thigh was bitten by a trained attack dog. A robber used his dog to intimidate his victims. He went to the ER for treatment of the wound and a tetanus shot. A judge ordered the Doberman Pinscher to be destroyed.

November 1978: Mike was once again greeted by familiar medical personnel in the ER. While Mike's black-and-white was stopped to allow pedestrians to cross, a drunk driver had crashed into his rear end. An altercation ensued when making the arrest. A laymen's diagnosis would be whiplash. Mike sustained a lumbar sprain and a cervical strain. Tests revealed that the neck injury had a partial compromise of the right axillary nerve. The hospital provided a neck brace. Since Shriner's Hospital designed apparatus for disabled children, they were contacted to design a back brace for Mike. A special lumbar support was needed to accommodate Mike's ileostomy.

CHAPTER 21

The Return of the Bad Penny (1978)

A September newspaper article was titled "Girl Raped Seeking Room." It stated that a fifteen-year-old girl was raped Wednesday afternoon when she visited the home of an acquaintance. In connection with the incident, Vern was charged with First Degree Sexual Assault and Risk of Injury to a Minor. Police said the girl was assaulted when she visited Vern's home to look at a room that she was thinking of renting. Vern, "the bad penny," had reappeared.

A prosecutor's report summarized: "At 1730 hours detectives were stopped on Main Street by the victim, Beatrice, and her boyfriend, Wilbur. He informed the detectives that his girlfriend had been raped by the owner of an auto repair shop. The victim stated that she knew the man worked at the repair shop near her home, but she did not know the man's name. Beatrice also told them that she did not know the address of the house where he had taken her, but she could show the policemen how to get there. Detectives were shown a house on Anderson Street. They discovered the name of the person who resides there to be Vern. At the repair shop, the victim identified Vern, a black male (age 36) as the person who had sexually assaulted her."

Vern was transported to the police department by Detective Paul and his partner. Detectives Edwardo and Charlie escorted the victim, who was accompanied by her older sister. Within the detective division, Beatrice was interviewed by Detective Edwardo. Her statement indicated that she had left her home on Main Street at approximately 1:30 PM and was walking to her cousin's when she observed the accused in a brown Pinto. Knowing him to be from the repair shop, she spoke to him and asked if he knew of any place where she could rent a room. The accused stated that he had a room at his house and that she could look at it. The victim agreed. Upon their arrival, Vern showed her throughout the house. While in the living room, he offered Beatrice some marijuana. They both smoked it. Vern then went into a bedroom and returned with a small brown bottle. He told Beatrice it was cocaine and gave her some.

Beatrice affirmed that when she began to get high, Vern asked her to have sex with him. She refused. Vern then gave her some wine to drink. Soon he took her into the bedroom, placed her upon the bed and tried to remove her clothes. She again rejected his advances. He relented just long enough to remove all of his own clothing. He then held her down while he raised her blouse and sucked her breast. The victim declared that Vern then forced her to have oral sex—pulling her by the hair and pushing her mouth upon him. She also stated that Vern placed some cocaine in her vagina in order to suck it from her. This foreplay lasted about a half hour before he finally put his penis into her vagina and had an orgasm within her.

After he had finished with her, Beatrice went into the bathroom. He entered and gave her thirty dollars in cash. The victim went on to say that as she was leaving, Vern stopped her and took back the thirty dollars but offered her a ride home. She refused. Beatrice walked home, located her boyfriend and told him about the incident. Then they both went to the repair shop and confronted Vern, who tried to give them money. Both refused the money and left the shop. That was when they saw the detectives.

The victim finished her statement by describing Vern's home—the color of his couch, details about the bathroom, the number of televisions, a small bed in the bedroom, a den with a table, a stereo and mirrors on the wall. (This information confirmed the fact that she had been in Vern's home.) The detective's report ended: "The victim was treated at the hospital."

In room 2 of the detective division, Detective Charlie read the accused his constitutional rights. Vern signed not only a statement verifying knowledge of those rights, but a waiver as well. He was then questioned. The interview produced Vern's version of the incident: He had been on his way home at approximately 1:30 PM when he observed Beatrice standing on the corner of Main and Allen. Vern stated that she asked him for a ride, but he informed her that he was only going to his house to pick something up. She allegedly said that she didn't care—she needed a ride to get away from her boyfriend. When they arrived at his home, she supposedly asked to borrow thirty dollars. When Vern asked her what she was going to do for him, Beatrice answered she could show him a good time—have sex with him. The accused went on to say that because she took out a "rubber" for him to use, he got the impression that she had VD, so he did not have sex with her. Instead, he asked if she wanted a ride home. She replied, "No, I'll walk." She then left the house. The accused reiterated that at no time did he have sex with the victim.

Vern claimed that on occasion, he had loaned Beatrice money from his place of business. (She lived near his garage.)

The accused also added that Beatrice had told him that she was "hustling" on the block because she needed money.

Vern was arrested for Sexual Assault, but there would never be a trial. The victim disappeared! Mike believed that Vern was responsible. He only hoped that she had merely been scared away—that no further harm had come to her. (Mike was not personally involved in this case, but the incident serves as an example of Vern's character—or lack thereof.)

CHAPTER 22

Self-Taught (1978)

Mike had received different types of driver training: motorcycle, class-two trucks and high-speed cruiser techniques. But he had no experience with heavy-duty equipment, like the thirty-ton power shovel now traveling down Main Street with no driver! He was about to become self-taught. My poem explains what happened:

A Strange Happening

It was an amazingly quiet spring evening,
Until kids completed hot-wire engineering.

A 30-ton power shovel they set meandering,
At 10 mph from where it had been standing.

Without a driver, down Main Street it kept coming.
It was all up to Mike. He had to do something!

He'd have to jump the wide tread constantly moving.
Should he miss, the possibility was frightening.

Reaching the cab, he experimented with steering.
While the amazed eyes of onlookers kept peering.

Everybody's property needed protecting,
So, the correct lever he had best be selecting!

If damage was suffered, people would be faulting,
This police officer for the beast not halting.

The aggressor was the recipient of Mike's cussing,
As he viewed parked cars it would soon be crushing.

Frantically pulling and pushing this lever and that,
The approaching predator finally slowed 'til it just sat.

Only inches away the autos remained gleaming:
No scrapes, no dents, no radiators leaking.

For a minute Mike stayed there, just simply staring,
His expression belying no worry or caring.

But very soon, a tiny smile was revealing,
The relief that would send his laughter pealing.

Mike's audience suddenly erupted with clapping. All had been entertained by this strange happening!

A newspaper article showed Mike sitting in the bulldozer. There would be no lack of thrilling adventures! Over the course of Mike's career, he would experience dangers in every permutation: bullets, vehicles, knives, bricks, broken bottles, men, women and even a peer.

CHAPTER 23

Morale (August 1979)

The newspaper's page-one story was titled "Lack of Manpower Weighs on Police." There were constantly huge backlogs of calls. The story told of an eight-year police veteran who became so frustrated that he pulled his cruiser to the curb and radioed his commander, "I quit." The article declared that he was only one of seven policemen who had turned in their badges within the last month.

The reporter specified that manpower had dwindled from 500 several years ago to 379. He declared, "The city council voted to hire thirty more officers, but by the time they are trained and sworn in (not until spring), an estimated attrition rate of eighteen added to recruit dropouts would make the seemingly large addition become, in reality, an addition of only eight."

The story showed insight when it proclaimed, "The increasing work load is making officers battle-weary and therefore increases physical injuries and mental stress." The reporter's figures indicated that twenty-four officers were now off duty because of work-related injuries. It was his belief that the shortage began in 1975, when the city enacted a budget freeze on hiring. Since then, 130 had retired, resigned, or been dismissed.

He quoted the chief who believed that 440 officers would be *adequate* (sixty fewer than years ago)! Overtime had already proven to be a poor solution for the vacancies.

An important councilman declared, "Due to all the other priorities of the city, thirty new officers are all that's possible." (Reconstruction of the civic center was his priority.) Other councilmen promised to expand the police department to 440 by **next July**!

The reporter had interviewed forty-five officers and found that manpower was only one cause for low morale. Others included the following:

1. Infighting among top commanders.
2. Division of the city into five separate districts. (Backup cruisers from one district were not allowed to enter an adjoining district to help a fellow officer.)
3. Lack of leadership from the chief.
4. Disappointment because of the recent arrest of three police officers.

Neighborhood groups finally exerted enough pressure upon the city council that they ordered the city manager to investigate allegations of poor morale. They gave him two weeks to identify the problem. If he should fail, then a corporate-funded group or a hired outsider would be used. I thought, *Save the city's meager purse! I'll give you the answers.*

Gentlemen,

Let it be understood: There is a rampant disease within the police department. The disease may be diagnosed as "No Morale" and, just like cancer, it has many different causes. Since research must ensue before treatment can be prescribed, I offer you my notes:

1. ***The ultra-liberal stance of the administration*** *infects citizens with low resistance. They begin to believe that their right to pursue happiness is supreme and that their responsibility towards others is nonexistent. Certain city councilmen prefer to make excuses for these criminals rather than to take appropriate action. These same politicians are bringing great pressure upon the chief of police.*

   Ultra-liberalism must be treated with a dose of conservatism. Every person must ingest all of the laws, and the police must be allowed to dispense equal justice. To oversee these treatments, a competent police chief is needed. Such a person can be found within the ranks of your own police department. He holds a doctorate in "Street Experience". (His background will induce the patrolmen's respect.) I understand the outsider now being considered merely holds a "Desk Jockey's" degree.

2. ***A severe manpower shortage*** *exposes officers to three or four extra shifts per week. One-man cruisers are permitted even in the most dangerous districts. Good citizens vent their ire upon these*

*overworked officers because of slow ser-
vice or no service. Officers are insecure
about adequate back-up units. They are
frustrated that they cannot do their jobs
right! All of this causes fatigue, injury,
hypertension, family stress, apathy and
depression. Since the city cannot afford
the antidote (a full complement—121
more officers), perhaps rest is the next
best treatment. A twelve-hour day with
a four-day work week would allow
amenable overtime. One of the days
during the three-day work break could
be used to equally distribute mandatory
overtime, yet an officer would still have
a two-day work break. Those officers
willing to obtain even more overtime
or extra private jobs have those two
remaining off-days in which to secure
work by union seniority. None would
be subjected to working double-shifts
(sixteen hours straight) as they are now
doing.*

*Because inadequate staffing is a
chronic disorder, it can only be controlled with continuous treatment. The
department must be allowed to recruit
on a regular basis. As a head nurse
in the emergency room has admitted,
"The presence of eager student nurses,
instead of impairing patient care, has
improved patient care by reminding*

the senior staff that those patients are people." So too, new rookies could give the department the shot in the arm that it needs to prevent callused apathy.

3. **The malignancy of the racist police group known as the Guardians** *should be excised. Its original purpose, that of a social group, has metastasized into a political action group which sympathizes only with blacks. White officers requesting membership have been denied. Any proclamation of its need is negated by the existence of two non-racist representative groups: the Police Union and the Police Benevolent Association. Each organization sepa-rately fulfills* **all needs of all officers**.

4. **Compensation benefits are unreli-able.** *Medical payments and the offi-cer's reimbursements are predicted to take 4–6 weeks, but often take 4–6 months (longer if city hall loses one's receipts). This causes the city to have bad credit with pharmacies and medi-cal supply companies; the injured offi-cer is forced to pay for his needs from his own pocket and hope for reimburse-ment. The compensation bureaucracy must be simplified.*

5. **The empty gymnasium and the lack of physical fitness program** *is detrimental to officers as well as those*

citizens they are supposed to protect. Physical fitness should be mandatory, and programs should be scheduled within the regular work week. Experts from the YMCA could help develop personalized programs for each officer. Now, even those officers who are willing to exercise on their own time have no equipment available. (An ounce of prevention is worth a pound of cure.)

6. ***A complete history is needed for a proper diagnosis.*** *How better to review a case than with the patient himself. But the department is maintained by military status, thus a patrolman's opinion may never reach the top brass. I therefore suggest an anonymous questionnaire be distributed at each squad's roll call. Include such questions as:*

   a. *What problems are you encountering on the job? Can you suggest solutions.*

   b. *Have you recently required a lawyer? If so, did you choose the police representative? If yes, were you satisfied?*

   c. *Would you use the gym if exercise equipment were provided?*

   Because the city manager has said that he wishes to approach this problem in a positive manner, I have tried to

*suggest realistic solutions. As the dep-
uty mayor would like proof that there
is a morale problem, I give professional
testimony as a veteran consultant—for
I am the wife of one of those affected
(infected) police officers. Since the
mayor would like to bring this problem
out into the open, I am sending a copy
of this letter to the newspaper and every
councilman.*

*This disease has become epidemic.
It not only affects police officers and
their families, but the city's residents,
working commuters and even its visi-
tors. All are affected and they need your
immediate attention.*

*With hopes that this problem is
not merely used as a political football
in this election year, I remain...*
A HOPEFUL WIFE

I decided it would be wise to remain anonymous to both
my husband and to city officials. I did, however, freely dispense
my own medicine, TLC (tender loving care). This chronic
morale problem affected our lives for some time. Eventually,
other organizations helped by donating equipment for the
gymnasium. City administrators acknowledged the problem
and replaced the police chief. Winter would cause a minimal
slowdown in crime, and the long recruitment procedure would
begin.

In October 1979, the force was still shorthanded, so Mike was sent alone to investigate a disturbance call. He experienced a "sucker punch," which was so powerful that it knocked Mike unconscious. He entered the ER with a broken nose, a chipped tooth and a scratched left cornea. He left the hospital with an eye patch and a brace over his nose. Mike's own dentist would have to cap the tooth.

CHAPTER 24

Goal (1979)

In my role as a mother, I bestowed total devotion. In my role as a school bus driver, I gave loyal dedication. In my role as a union steward, I extended enormous energy. In my role as a wife, I granted unconditional love. For myself, I began to realize that I had given little. This truth is made evident in my poem:

Restless

The midnight shifts are such a bore,
For loneliness is what's in store;
There's time to thoughtfully explore,
If life should have offered me more.

With daughter and girlfriend in bed;
Son sleeping out—hope he's been fed.
Now alone, thoughts fill up my head,
With things I should probably shed!

But they refused to be deleted;
I wonder, "Have I been cheated?"

"Have my options been depleted?"
"Are my responsibilities completed?"

Sleeping in late, until daylight,
Has been a joy these past five nights,
While on vacation from six AM flights,
To my job, driving school tikes.

When working, there's no time for psyche;
Nor the goal considered this night.
But, I'll keep my decision in sight.
*An autobiography I **will** someday write!*

It will bring understanding sought,
From family, I've placed aloft.
As weariness comes from this page of thought,
Sleep should arrive. Ought it not?

CHAPTER 25

Internal Affairs (1980)

On March 31, 1980, Sergeant Alfred of the police department's Internal Affairs Division received a five-page complaint. "**Undue Harassment**" charges were being filed against Officer Michael. Guess who filed? Vern was back in our lives again!

Vern's complaint read: "This complaint concerns undue harassment by Officer Michael dating back from 1971 until the last incident on March 18, 1980. After nine years of harassment by one man, I feel that I must come forward and speak out against this man making threats against my life and trying to stop me from making any progress in this society."

My diary clearly notes my reaction: *I am appalled by this lowlife who has the audacity to try and use the legal system **against** my husband. As I read Vern's complaint, I was amazed by both his outright lies and his expertise in telling half-truths. I really should not have been surprised, for I'd previously read his 1978 work of art—his fictitious version of the rape of a fifteen-year-old girl.*

Since IAD (Internal Affairs Division) must investigate all complaints (no matter the source), Mike was asked to answer each accusation. The investigating supervisor labeled them A through N. To allow easy comprehension, each allegation was

105

registered, and Mike's corresponding rebuttal immediately follows in bold print:

A) Vern: The first incident occurred in the <u>summer</u> of 1971. I was driving along Allen Avenue when I was stopped by Officer Michael and another officer. I was asked to get out of the car for <u>no apparent reason</u>. I didn't get right out of the car when they asked me to. One officer was on the passenger side of the car and Officer Michael was on the driver's side. My doors were locked, and my <u>window</u> was down because I was trying to listen to what was being said. Officer Michael told me again to get out of the car and in the process, <u>he put his hand inside the car and tried to pull me out</u>. When this happened, <u>I tried to drive off</u> and <u>later understood</u> that Officer Michael, by getting <u>his hand caught</u> in the window of the car, had been <u>dragged for a brief moment</u>. His hand had been caught because by the nature of his actions, which were unwarranted at the time, and being unsure of their intentions, I put the window up, and it caught Officer Michael's <u>hand</u>. I went home because I <u>had to take care of a few things there</u>. It was very <u>important that I not go to jail that night</u>. Officer Michael <u>somehow had gotten a warrant</u> for my arrest. I pleaded guilty to the charges brought against me and was given a sentence of 1 to 5 years, which was suspended after I served one year and three months.

Mike: This incident did not occur in the summer but on December 9, 1971 at approx-

imately 11:30 PM in freezing weather. All the windows were down as he was driving, not just the driver's window for the purpose of talking to me. He was not stopped for 'no apparent reason.' He had run several red lights while traveling west on Allen Avenue. My relief partner was aware that Vern's license was under suspension, so he came around to the driver's side of the car to check the license that Vern had handed me. It was Officer Edgar who first asked Vern to step from his vehicle because the license belonged to Vern's brother. (At that time, it was a crime to drive without a license and the driver could be arrested.) Vern states that only my hand was caught in the window, and supposedly, this was without his knowledge. My entire arm was extended into the car, reaching for the shifting lever in an attempt to push it up into park and to turn off the key. I was dragged approximately 60 feet which even at his accelerated speed took more than one moment. (He fled from the scene. The few things he had to take care of were probably the disposal of drugs from his car.)

B) Vern: When I got out of prison, Officer Michael kept <u>sending me messages</u> through my brother, that he was going to get me and that I had better leave town and that if I didn't it was going to be bad for me. I left town and went to New York and worked there for a while. I returned to this city thinking things had cooled down and that I had to come back and start all over again. I felt that I had paid for my crime, even though it was <u>not inten-</u>

tional. Since returning, I have started my present auto repair business.

Mike: I am aware that Vern has a brother that looks like him as do 100 other alert police officers. I was first made aware of this by Officer Edgar who informed me that he uses his brother's license to drive. I have never written or sent messages to his brother and would like to see these items of fiction. The dragging was intentional, as was proven in a court of law. (One has to wonder how he got his New York money with which he returned to buy the repair shop.)

C) Vern: Upon my release from prison, the front page of the newspaper carried a story in reference to the incident between myself and Officer Michael which I just described above. The article stated that the incident which had occurred, and which had prompted Officer Michael to file a suit (Item D) against me was the first of its kind where a police officer filed a suit against a private citizen from incidents which took place in the officer's line of duty.

Mike: I am aware of a small newspaper article printed in January 1974. Because it was given to me, I'm not sure if it was found on the front page. It stated that a policeman had filed a $50,000 damage (Item D) suit in Superior Court. I had nothing to do with this article being published. Reporters have free access to court proceedings. I can't say that I have any regrets if the article was construed as a negative advertisement for his repair shop. The suit was

filed by my attorney because of my agreement with the compensation insurance company which sought reimbursement for the thousands of dollars for medical bills which they had already paid and will continue to pay for the rest of my life. (This included ileostomy supplies, medications and complications.)

D) Vern: Since filing that suit, Officer Michael has found pleasure in making my life miserable with his threats against my person and my property.

Mike: I have never threatened him. My attorney has sought a lien on his property to assure reimbursement to the compensation carrier and damages to me.

E) Vern: He has asked me on occasion who my insurance company was.

Mike: My lawyer has contacted his lawyer seeking such information. I have had no personal contact.

F) Vern: He has also asked whether, or not, I owned any property in my name because, as he stated to me, he was going to get everything I had.

Mike: My lawyer has sought this information from the registry of deeds. As to ownership of the auto repair shop, that has been fully advertised to all newspaper readers. His six-inch advertisement includes Vern's picture.

G) Vern: The next incident happened when Officer Michael came down to my place of business in 1977 to hold me on a warrant. While driving me to the station, Officer Michael said, "Vern, I know you don't have a license, and I know you drive without a license." Let it be known here that at the time of charging me with the aforementioned offense, that I was not operating a motor vehicle of any kind.

Mike: I did pick up Vern since officers are given warrants to serve within their assigned district. I don't recall if the year was 1977 or 1976, but the larceny warrant was for writing bad checks in another town. The incident about charging him for driving without a license when he was not driving is untrue. He was in a vehicle at the time I found him to serve the warrant. The charge of operating a motor vehicle while under suspension never went to court because the prosecutor felt that Vern would just produce four witnesses to testify that they were riding in the car at that time and that Vern was not the driver. Vern was alone at the time of the stop.

H) Vern: The next incident occurred when I was involved in an auto accident on Main Street. I was a passenger at the time of the accident. I was hurt badly in that accident. Somehow Officer Michael just happened to arrive at the scene. While waiting for help to arrive, I remember hearing Officer Michael say to another officer, that I was not hurt—just kidding. My body was racked with pain as I had broken three ribs and my kidneys were <u>fractured</u>. Even at a time such as this, this man still finds it within himself to harass me. During that night, while in the hospital, holding on to consciousness, Officer Michael came into my room saying things to me that I was unable to respond to because of the acute pain I was having.

Mike: I do remember Vern being involved in a motor vehicle accident at some time. I do not remember speaking to him or doing the investigation for it. I surely did not visit him at the hospital. If he believes I was there, he must have seen me in a bad dream caused by medication. When was this accident? At what hospital was he treated?

I) Vern: Another incident between myself and Officer Michael occurred when, according to Officer Michael, he had received complaints that my dog was attacking people on Windsor Street. He also alleges that when he responded to the complaints at my place of business, my dog also tried to attack him. Officer Michael shot my dog and killed him. Officer Michael did not inform me of this until the next morning after shooting the dog. I know that my dogs don't go out on the street attacking people. They are not attack dogs. They have always stayed within the confines of the garage where I conduct my business.

Mike: I am aware of a dog incident but do not know the date or time for I was not involved. I was told that an officer responded to a dog attacking citizens on North Chapel Street, and the dog was shot with the Lieutenant's approval. I was told that the dog did not die but was brought to a veterinarian. For all I know he is still alive. I was once bitten while on duty, but

**that attack incident was published in the news-
paper and had nothing to do with Vern's dog.**

J)   Vern: He mentioned something to do with immigration. I believe that Officer Michael is playing with my civil rights by saying I was wanted
for some sort of immigration violation when I
know I have not committed any crimes under the
Immigration Statutes, prompting Officer Michael
to make reference to my nationality.

**Mike: I never said anything about immi-
gration. Any information Vern was given about
immigration problems did not come from me.
However, I am <u>now</u> aware that he self-deported
back to Jamaica for a year in the '60s but I am
unaware of the circumstances.**

K)   Vern: The last incident occurred on March 18,
1980, when Officer Michael came to my garage
allegedly in response to a complaint of my threatening someone. Someone owed me some money,
and I went to collect what was owed to me. The
person who I went to see, rather than pay me what
was owed to me, decided to pull a knife on me
instead.

**Mike: Vern neglected to mention his use
of a crowbar at the time he approached the
<u>woman</u>.**

L)   Vern: I have a witness that can attest to this. When
this happened, I returned to my place of business.
Later that night, Officer Michael appeared at my
house requesting to see me. He said that I was
wanted for threatening someone and that it would
be best for me to come down to the station and

give myself up. I was to do this before 10:00 PM. If I was not down at the station before that time, I may as well not bother coming at all because he was going to get a warrant at 10:00 PM and come back and get me.

Mike: Another officer accompanied me to Vern's house. At his house we informed the unknown person who answered the door that Vern should give himself up that night, otherwise I would get a warrant. I have no knowledge of an alleged witness.

M) Vern: After leaving my home and his unsuccessful attempt to carry out his crusade against me, he came to my place of business searching for me. He came in saying I was wanted, and I should come down to the police station and give myself up and not make it hard for him and get a search warrant. I know I didn't do anything, and he had no right coming into my business the way he did.

Mike: We continued the search at Vern's place of business. I knocked on the door and observed Vern through the window. An unknown person opened the door. Vern made eye contact with me. The lights went out and Vern fled. Perhaps this unknown person standing in the doorway and turning off the lights would also be a witness for him. If he hadn't been involved, why did he flee?

N) Vern: Officer Michael was apparently working the 3-11 shift that night. At the end of his duty, he had two of his friends come back to my home later that night about 1:30 AM, again looking for me and saying they wanted to arrest me for making a threat against someone. They tried to gain entry into my home unlawfully but were not granted access. Again, it was stressed that if I turned myself in, it would make it easier on myself. I did not go because I knew that it would have been detrimental to me. As I said before, Officer Michael has made many threats against me, sending messages to me through my brother. He speaks of what he's going to do to me one day, and at this point I have to take caution because he's been threatening my life too much for too long, and I feel I must somehow prevent this man from committing a crime— taking my life. One day he will because he knows he's got the right to carry a gun and use it, and I don't know what he's planning or what may lie in store for me at any time.

Mike: I am unaware of any follow-up done by the next shift. By 1:30 AM, I was in another state, had drank four cans of beer and could care less about police work. Sex and sleeping were the only possible things on my mind. I can tell you that a judge signed an arrest warrant for this incident on April 4, 1980. In closing, the undersigned would like to say: 1.) I believe Vern instigated this complaint seeking to irritate me so that I will do something stupid to jeopardize any damage claims that I am now seeking. 2.) Every time he gets arrested, my civil suit against him is put aside. How can this help me? 3.) My suit is a private issue between myself, my attorney and the compensation insurance company.

4.) Since the 1971 incident the below officer has been intelligent enough to not confront Vern without a witness being present. The only exception to this was when no other officer was available to arrest him for operating a motor vehicle while his license was under suspension. 5.) This officer wishes to apply for a warrant for Vern charging him with Section 53a-157 and 53a-183 (Harassment). Please advise. (Mike was advised against this.)

Each accusation was further investigated by the Internal Affairs Division. Each was found to be invalid. Vern's falsities were not allowed to besmirch Mike's reputation, but they did rankle his disposition.

The fact that Mike was forced to waste his time responding to such garbage infuriated me. My diary registers my irritation and my fear: *The man has such gall! Should we fear other forms of unwarranted reprisal?*

CHAPTER 26

FTO (1980)

Mike became a Field Training Officer. His first trainee was a small rookie with only a twenty-inch waist from which to secure all necessary paraphernalia: gun belt, revolver, handcuffs, bullet case, radio, slapjack, nightstick and a chatelaine for keys. Because many policemen viewed the idea of female street-patrol personnel with antipathy, she was assigned to Mike. His judgment would be based on her capability.

She had a keen awareness of state and city statutes but wanted to know more. She was even contemplating advanced judo. As a female, she needed to excel because most male officers expected her to fail.

It was Mike's job to teach her everything he had learned on the street. He advised the following:

1. Get to know the people. Befriend the residents and understand their predicaments. Introduce yourself to business owners. Always pay for your meals. Be aware of the hookers, pimps and drug dealers.

2. Play the role of a political dilettanté so that you can become aware of who is a friend of law enforcement, and who just professes to be.
3. Recognize the affectations of the accused: innocent, haughty, grateful and indignant.
4. Be adaptable. During a shift, one can experience the monotony of door checks and crossing guard duty to a frenzied foot chase or a 10-0 call (officer needs help).
5. Never become complacent. Always be conscious of your surroundings. Never sit with your back to a restaurant door. When entering a room, survey its occupants. Always call in your location before approaching a traffic stop, and make sure your gun guard is unsnapped.
6. Interpret the statements of other officers. Cynical wit is merely an effort to make light of the true levity of a situation. A peer's sexist comment could be mere banter, which can be answered with a shake of the head. If the comment is repugnant, a snide rebuke may be necessary.
7. Think out of the box:
    a. Mike and his trainee were called to a domestic complaint. Upon arrival, spouses were found to be inebriated and quarrelsome. The officers were able to establish a truce, which eventually led the semi-soused consorts into a re-marriage ceremony performed by the self-ordained Reverend Michael (Officer Mike).
    b. Both Mike and his partner had their hands placed on the door handles as Mike slowly pulled their cruiser to a spot very close to a park picnic table. Sitting there was a group of black men who matched the description of a nearby mugging.

From his window, Mike asked a desultory question, "Have you seen any white guys run through here?" That ruse allowed the officers the few seconds needed. Mike tackled one as his partner subdued another. A back-up car picked up a third. Two women identified their assailants, and their pocketbooks were retrieved from under the table.

8. Immediately reject corruption. Depravity can become chronic and possibly terminal. Seductions come in many forms: business gratuities, outright bribes, sexual favors and political pressures. A bad cop is dangerous to his peers and to the public.

9. Practice Mike's Code—treat people decently:

    a. If you treat people nicely, there is a 75 percent chance that they will cooperate.

    b. The trainee was made aware of a previous kindness. A year ago, Mike was working a road construction site in the North End. A neighborhood child watched as repairs were being made to his street. After a while, he came close enough to talk with Mike. The boy eventually left. When he later returned, Mike gave him enough change to buy himself a soda. Now, one year later, Mike and his trainee were in that same neighborhood when a young teen approached. He asked Mike, "Do you remember me?" Not wanting to disappoint the boy, Mike replied, "You look familiar, but I don't know where I've seen you." The boy's bright smile indicated that he was about to share his secret. He happily announced, "I've grown a bit. Last year you gave me money to buy a soda. I just wanted to come over to say hello." Mike replied with his own smile. "Thank you, I'm glad you did."

c. Mike developed many bonds of humanity. When he arrested a young woman for shoplifting, he understood her criminal mistake. She needed to provide for herself and her small child. After she served a small sentence, Mike continued to stay in touch.

d. Mike's several ER trips allowed him to develop friendships. He encouraged one compassionate nurse to befriend an officer who was depressed after losing his family due to divorce. Her moral support built a friendship, which later progressed into marriage.

e. When sent to the hospital to transport a prisoner back to jail, the prisoner complained about feeling poorly. He stated, "I haven't eaten in several hours." Mike bent policy rules and pulled up to a drive-thru window. He bought the man a donut and a cup of coffee. Months later, Mike was thrilled to tell me about a stranger who had sought him out. The guy had told Mike, "I want you to know that I'm straightening out my life, and I wanted to thank you for your kindness. I will never forget that cup of coffee."

Both Mike and I enjoyed helping people. Over the years, I have been a Cub Scout den mother, a volunteer solicitor for the heart fund, a coordinator for a girls' softball league and the neighborhood organizer for Jerry Lewis muscular dystrophy tag sales.

CHAPTER 27

Safe (1980)

Wives of those police officers working B and C Squads (evening and night shifts) spend a lot of time alone. Perhaps so many officers marry nurses because they are acclimated to crazy work shifts too. For the many spouses who are living a normal day shift, the long nightly hours are lonely and sometimes frightening. (During those hours, a police wife is all too well aware that she is solely responsible for the safety of home, family and herself.)

Once a released criminal seemed to be following our family around an amusement park. Mike recognized the man who had once gone berserk in the police station. Mike had helped another officer wrestle him into handcuffs. Now unarmed, Mike certainly wanted no ruckus in front of our children. He informed me of pending danger and instructed me to continue acting as if I were enjoying myself. As an excuse to separate himself from us, he told our son and daughter that he was going to the bathroom and would meet up with us at the hot dog stand. I was to forestall them with a trip into the Fun House. As we entered, I glanced back to see the ruffian still coming our way.

Upon entering the men's room, Mike immediately took a position just to the left of the doorway, but the man never entered. Several minutes later, Mike exited to find that the parolee had disappeared. Apparently, the man had just happened to be walking in the same direction and never recognized Mike in civilian clothes.

After that nerve-racking experience, I no longer objected to Mike wearing a gun while he was off-duty. I also began to worry about such a person showing up at our house. What would I do if Mike was not there? I vented my fear about such a possibility by writing:

Alone at Night

> *"What's that?" Sitting upright, I opened my eyes as if that would help me to better hear! My foggy brain began to decipher the sounds: the high pitches were the rabies tag jingling against a dog license; the lower pitches were the flapping ears of our eleven-year-old German short-haired Pointer. Once I identified the sounds, the meaning was clear. It was just Thor! He had come into the bedroom and given me a gentle wake-up call. His old bladder couldn't always make it through the night. As my bare feet hit the cool floor, I was relieved that the floor wasn't wet! Grateful that my friend had awakened me in time, I assured, "Okay boy. I'll let you out."*
>
> *As I passed the kitchen stove my eyes squinted against the clock's bright digital numbers glaring 3:30 AM. "Mike's usually home by now!" (His "Task Force" detail worked 6:00 PM*

to 2:00 AM.) Thor and I proceeded through the kitchen, the mud room, the back door and across the yard to the kennel. Suddenly, a chill streaked down my spine. I wasn't sure if its cause was a sudden breeze or a feeling of foreboding. I shivered again but immediately reproached myself, "Don't be stupid. The entire back yard is fortified by a six-foot-high stockade fence. If anyone is lurking in the darkness, Thor would be barking." It was with false confidence that I reminded myself, "Besides, vengeful lunatics would never think that Mike lived so far away from his work. The department doesn't give out officers' addresses, and we are not listed in the phone book." Even with these safeguards, I found myself scrupulously surveying the entire area. I decided not to make the trek back across the lawn alone. When a wagging tail demonstrated his gratitude for his relief, we then made the trip back together.

My last soft pats reassured me. The physical contact gave me confidence. I felt safe because of him. On my command, "Stay," Thor immediately reestablished himself as a door sentry. Indeed, I was safe.

I made my way back to the empty double bed. Its flannel sheet would provide physical comfort, but psychological comfort would have to come from pleasant thoughts. I pictured Thor's motorized tail when he heard Mike's car, and I envisioned Mike's smile as he was greeted by the only family member who was up at that wee hour. After years of private nightly liaisons, they had developed an extraordinary friendship. In my mind, I covertly joined them for their walk and then watched as they played a quiet game of catch in the backyard. A smile came to my face as I imagined Thor and Mike just sitting together, talking—or not. (I believe this canine can actually read Mike's mind.) "What a loyal pet. Pet? Hell—he's a part of our family!"

I nodded off to sleep with one last satisfying thought, "In fact, he's the head of the household—the ultimate protector of Michael, his home and his f...a...m...i...l...y."

My diary confession: *Our dog alleviates a lot of my fear. Only Thor knows I am not as brave as I pretend.*

CHAPTER 28

A Pretty Good Year (1980)

1980 was a pretty good year. Mike only sustained two injuries. In July, Mike was struggling to remove a surly drunk from a Civic Center event. When they both went down, Mike hit his left knee on the edge of a cement step. The doctor at the police clinic misjudged Mike's endurance for pain. He did not order an x-ray. Mike was sent home wearing an ace bandage and was instructed to apply ice. After several days, Mike returned to work still wearing an ace bandage. The knee remained painful for weeks. The next time he injured that same knee, it **was** x-rayed. Mike was surprised when that doctor asked, "When did you fracture your kneecap?" (The x-ray showed a healed fracture.) The city clinic had misdiagnosed his previous injury.

Mike was vice president of the Police Benevolent Association. In December 1980, he and other officers went to visit a special needs facility to distribute fifty Christmas gifts. As a male patient approached, Mike gave him a smile. In return, the patient unexpectedly kicked Mike's right ankle (the one that had undergone a ligament transfer). The case worker profusely apologized and explained, "He just does that." After that, Mike wore lace-up combat boots while on duty and cowboy boots when off-duty.

Besides his benevolent work, Mike was asked to organize the department's Youth Explorer Program.

CHAPTER 29

Jousting for Turf (1981)

Mike was sorry that he had volunteered for this overtime. Working a day shift was damned hot! The heat could be seen rising from the city's pavement, yet there he sat on the fender of his cruiser—seemingly enjoying a picnic lunch. The sun's sizzling rays wilted the lettuce in his sandwich, but he remained cooler than his dill cucumber. He deserved an Academy Award for this performance!

News had been transmitted through the streets that Mike needed to be "taken down". Fernando had declared himself the man to do it. He ruled this neighborhood and would not tolerate any interference from cops. Mike had received the message. If he did not reply, he would be perceived as a coward. Mike had to make it known that he could not be intimidated. A reticent cop would never gain the respect needed to do effective police work in this tough locale. Mike deemed today's broad daylight a good time for their joust. That was why his cruiser was now parked right in front of Fernando's tenement.

When a young boy approached, Mike acknowledged him with a smile. "Hi. *Como sé llama?*"

"Ernesto," he answered and quickly added, "You shouldn't be here. Fernando is looking for you." Mike was not surprised by the boy's awareness. Children learned very early the ways of the street.

"So I've heard," Mike replied as he reached into his pants pocket.

"Here's a buck. Go upstairs and see if he's home. If he is, tell him Officer Mike paid you to bring him a message." (Mike did not want the lout to think that this child was either his lackey or his friend. The boy would be safe if Fernando knew the child was just trying to make some money.)

Although reluctant, the desire for that dollar influenced Ernesto's decision. He grabbed a firm hold upon the bill as Mike instructed, "Tell him if he's got something to say to me, now is the time. I'm here waiting."

Shortly after Ernesto entered the building, Mike looked up to find a fuming Fernando staring down at him. Mike feigned an appearance of nonchalance and returned to his lunch. Actually, he was quite tense as he awaited his opponent. Fernando was taking his sweet time to consider Mike's surreptitious challenge. He was probably contemplating Mike's delightful beating but was hesitant to select such action. Backup could be waiting around the corner. Mike knew Fernando would check that out from his fire escape. Seeing none, he would question why Mike exuded so much self-confidence. He would be wondering just how good Mike could fight. He might even be pondering if Mike was a black belt.

Surely Mike's sitting there (an open target) suggested the possibility of a sniper's bullet. But hopefully his antagonist would consider what hell his life would be if the bullet was not fatal. He must be asking himself, "Is this cop nuts?" Mike hoped that Fernando would decide affirmatively to that question. That conclusion would render this lord wary of Mike and balance the situation: Fernando wanted Mike to be afraid of him; Mike wanted Fernando to be equally apprehensive.

Mike finally took one last sip of his Coke, slowly collected his trash and got back into his black-and-white. Apparently, his adversary decided to forfeit. Mike sighed with relief. Neither he nor his bulletproof vest had been tested.

"How was your day?" I inquired when he got home.

"Good," he answered. "But I think tomorrow will be better."

The hint of a smug smile inspired me to ask, "How so?"

After Mike reviewed the encounter, I responded with a slow shake of my head and pronounced the affirmation, "You **are** crazy."

"It helps," he simply replied. Then he gave me a quick peck on the nose and left the kitchen to take a shower. His intentionally speedy exit gave me no chance for rebuttal.

I returned my attention to the carrots I had been dicing. After my frustration was spent on them, I began to think about an effective strategy. Mike had to be reminded that he was not invincible. I was not about to let him fall victim to the "John Wayne syndrome" that we wives had been warned about. He needed to exercise more caution! Suddenly, I thought of something that would surely elicit his undivided attention. I quietly opened the bathroom door, slowly slid Mike's bath towel from the rack and tightly twirled it between my hands. Standing at the ready, I awaited the perfect moment to let it snap. Soon the shower door would be opening, and I would make my point!

CHAPTER 30

Injuries (1981)

January 9, 1981: On a very cold, icy day, a school crossing guard called out, and Mike was sent to replace her. During his tour, he slipped on the ice and sprained his bad ankle. It developed a ganglion cyst. He returned to work three weeks later.

February 24, 1981: Mike was sent alone to a domestic complaint. Since a woman's screams could be heard, Mike chose not to wait for backup. The irate abuser answered Mike's knock. He threw open the door and charged. Mike was immediately sent backward and over the second-floor railing. He landed in the first-floor lobby. Two backup officers arrived just in time to see Mike fall. While Mike lay unconscious, they made the arrest. An ER doctor diagnosed a mild concussion and ordered rest. Extra-strength Tylenol was in great demand.

September 4, 1981: A stress test produced high blood pressure during exertion. Mike began taking prescribed medication.

CHAPTER 31

Interdepartmental Memorandum (1982)

An official police department memorandum was issued by the commander of the Management Service Division. It named personnel who were being appointed to serve on a commendations review committee. Selected were one captain, one lieutenant, one sergeant, one detective and one patrolman (Mike).

I thought that Mike would be honored by this appointment, but I very quickly discovered that he was opposed to it! "Why?" I asked. "You'll be able to assure that good officers receive the credit they deserve."

Mike agreed that every exceptional performance deserved recognition, but he was acutely aware of the existing problems that hindered that goal. He explained, "Not every heroic act is noticed. Singling out just a few brings disappointment to other deserving officers." One of Mike's own personal experiences served as an excellent example. His name had not been submitted for commendation because of a simple oversight.

While on patrol, Mike and a relief partner discovered smoke billowing from an apartment building. They notified dispatch, then entered the burning building to evacuate its residents. Mike told me, "The heat was intense, and the smoke was horrible. My partner was overcome on the first floor, so I had to drag him out of the building. As I was waving to an arriving ambulance, an evacuated resident told me that there was a child still up on the third floor. So I went back in. My lungs were burning, and I had to force myself not to panic. I reached the apartment and found a small boy. The fire forced us out onto the back porch. Fortunately, a fire escape on an adjacent building was nearby, so I told him 'Hang on tight.' Then I leaped to get away from the flames. I made entry into that building by braking a corridor window. I carried the boy through the building and down to the street. No one noticed our exit from that adjacent building."

In the meantime, fire trucks had set up their equipment, and a police supervisor had reached the scene. A paramedic could only inform the sergeant of what he had been told: "His officer had succumbed to smoke while trying to rescue residents from the burning building." Since the recovering patrolman, himself, did not know how he had reached the street, the supervisor never found out about Mike's involvement. Therefore, he was the only one recommended for a commendation.

It did not bother Mike too much. After all, the other patrolman had entered the burning building. But when the time came to congratulate the recipient, Mike jokingly informed him, "Sure, I save your ass and you get the award!" Only then did that patrolman learn what Mike had done for him!

Besides oversights, there were other complications which caused the omission of deserving nominees. One supervisor expected excellence and considered it merely a part of every officer's job, so he gave no recommendations. Another supervisor played favorites and recommended only those officers who were easily commanded. A lazy supervisor did not want to be bothered with the additional paperwork required for documentation and recommendation. Another supervisor who was blessed with an exceptional squad did not want to choose just one officer from among all of his good men.

Even though Mike expressed his aversion to serving on the review committee, his resignation was not accepted. While serving on the committee, he assured that only exceptional endeavors were lauded. Since he and the appointed captain voted "yes" only on the truly extraordinary reviews, replacements were soon found for both of them!

Sometime later, Mike received a memorandum about a commendation medal of his own. He was to receive it for heroic effort extended in capturing drive-by murderers. Mike had been working Squad B on a dreadfully hot summer's night. Even though he patrolled a portion of the city's crime-ridden North End, staffing shortages caused him to man the district's cruiser alone. Turning onto Main Street, he observed a vehicle just two car lengths in front of him. It was slowing down at the intersection where pedestrians were gathered. (Groups were not unusual on that corner because the grocery store was a regular hangout.) Suddenly, fire flashes exploded from the right side of the car. The streaks of light indicated two handguns firing toward the people. Everyone was taking cover—falling to the sidewalk. Bullets sprayed the area. Four shots pierced the wall of the building, another dented an electrical box on a light pole. Then the car sped away from the intersection.

Mike knew that his first duty was to give first aid to any possible victims, but he also knew that the assailants would escape unless he immediately engaged in hot pursuit. It took only a moment for Mike to rationalize that another district's line unit was just a couple of blocks away. (In this part of the city, one cruiser's district was very small.) Mike's right foot floored the accelerator as his right hand activated the siren, triggered the strobe light switch, then grabbed for the radio. Mike called in that shots had been fired and gave the location of the shooting incident. He relayed that he did not know if anyone had been hit, but he requested immediate backup to verify any injuries. (Later he would discover that a twenty-two-year-old man had taken one bullet in a leg, another man had been struck in his arm and a third man had been instantly killed.)

Mike described the car: an old dark four-door with an out-of-state license plate. (He would later find out that it was a stolen vehicle.) Mike also announced the direction of their travel. Not wanting to relinquish his airwave, he continued pressing upon his microphone button. This gave him uninterrupted communication with the dispatcher, whom he updated at every turn. As the chase zigzagged across the city and up onto the highway, shots were constantly fired at Mike from both sides of the assailants' vehicle. By the time they exited into the South End of the city, Mike's front windshield had ben ventilated. One bullet had made a direct hit, creating a hole; another shot had ricocheted off the glass merely leaving a crack. The long race ended abruptly as the stolen vehicle reached a dead end. Their car came to a screeching stop. Four men bailed out of the car. Three scattered in different directions. Only one, the party exiting from the right rear, held his ground to shoot at Mike one more time. Without hesitation, Mike struck the man with his cruiser but applied his brakes at the exact moment of impact. This technique kept the guy from ending up under the cruiser—out of sight. The shooter's body went airborne, and his gun went flying onto the hood of the black-and-white. Mike exited his vehicle with gun in hand and hair raised at the back of his neck. Thoughts fled through his mind about the others, who were out there in the darkness. *From which direction would the bullet come? Where the hell was his backup?* Finally, it became apparent that the fleeing "homies" had decided to save themselves. Mike had to dodge no more bullets.

When backup units did arrive, they apologized for the brief delay and explained that their tardiness was caused by a communication problem. Mike had chased the perpetrators into the South End where a different radio channel was used. In the chaos, Mike never had time to switch his radio channel to the frequency used by their cruisers on that side of town. Therefore, these officers could not hear the chase. They had to await relayed instructions as their own dispatcher sent out secondhand information.

Mike's excitement produced an adrenaline rush. This natural high provided an ecstatic thrill. It was exhilarating to feel indestructible! It was overwhelming to overcome the bad guys—to render a little justice. Before the end of Mike's shift, the remaining parties were found.

I would be awakened twice that night. The first was hearing Mike enter the house during the wee hours of the morning. His normal routine would be to raid the refrigerator and then talk to his dog while he devoured a snack and a beer. But tonight, he came straight into the bedroom, so I was immediately concerned. "Are you all right?"

In the dark, I heard the squeak of his leather gun belt as he laid it upon the chair. "Yeah, I'm fine," he answered as he sat on the side of the bed and leaned toward me. "But I had one hell of a night!" I perceived an urgency from his ardent kiss and tried to interrogate him between more compelling kisses. From the bits and pieces he sparingly shared, I began to picture the high-speed chase with bullets flying—at my husband!

"God, you could have been killed!" The possibility incited my own wanton response, and I showed him how glad I was that he was still alive. I enjoyed the excess energy that was still pumping through Mike's veins, and together we cherished life completely.

Two hours after our lovemaking, I was awoken again. Beside me, Mike lay fitfully sleeping. I hugged him and whispered, "Shh—Go to sleep." He never woke to my words, but he did become calm. Even so, I held him close until the morning.

A memorandum now informed Mike that political dignitaries would be giving him a medal. A special ceremony was to be held at City Hall. Because of Mike's ego, he never received his medal! As the incident was regaled, the politicians took advantage of the media hype. To Mike, the political arena so tainted the whole affair that he told his supervisor he was not coming into the city on his day off just to be used by the city's politicians. The ordered commendation was rescinded!

All were convicted of both Murder and Conspiracy to Commit Murder upon the pedestrians, but prosecutors never pursued charges on behalf of the endangered officer.

Mike did receive one more memorandum regarding this case. He was notified of a pending civil suit. The first apprehended party was suing Mike for excessive force! He complained that Mike purposefully hit him with a vehicle and broke his leg. The judge dismissed the case and apologized to Mike for the inconvenience of attending court on his day off.

CHAPTER 32

The Pit (1982)

In July 1982, Mike engaged in a nighttime foot chase. The suspect had a bit of a head start, and Mike was disadvantaged by pounds of police paraphernalia around his waist. He would have to give it his all.

The area was a construction site where old brick buildings were being demolished. Mike last viewed the man as he flew around the corner of a partial teardown. Mike was at top speed when he reached that same corner. As he made the turn, it suddenly became pitch-black! All the rear floodlights had been broken long ago. A couple more steps sent Mike propelling into an open cellar pit.

An ER doctor diagnosed a bruised tendon on his right elbow. Tennis elbow would be the last injury sustained while in uniform.

CHAPTER 33

From Silver to Gold (1982)

Imagine being a homicide detective like a TV star on *N.Y.P.D.*—a nicely dressed investigator who receives substantial pay for an interesting job, an officer who possesses great power and who enjoys respect from decent society. In November 1982, Officer Mike turned in his silver patrolman's badge in exchange for a gold detective badge. (Detective Mike would soon discover that the world of a real detective is not nearly as wonderful as the version on TV.)

Mike found out that his detective's pay did not equal his actual on-duty hours. When the city's coffer was miniscule, overtime was compensated with "comp time". Extra hours were credited so that, in the future, the detective may receive equal off-hours upon his request. But requests were denied whenever the department declared it to be an inopportune time. Hours of owed compensation time accumulated into days. Overtime was only paid in cash (at time and a half) when important people were involved. For example, when a police-band radio was stolen from the mayor's private car, overtime wages were allowed! Overtime was restricted from Mike's prostitute murder case.

No amount of any type compensation could ever match the actual hours spent on a case. When Mike went off-duty physically, he remained on-duty mentally. In his mind, he continued to review all the things still needed to be done. He made mental lists (often notes) about witnesses to be found, interviews to be conducted and evidence to be secured. His brain spontaneously filtered the cacophony of statements, which had already been documented. For him, there was no time-off. Surcease came only when a case was solved.

The job was interesting! Both victims and perpetrators came from all classes. Crime scenes were diverse. Weapons were dissimilar and evidence was illusive. But the job was also horrific! It was totally unappealing when the odor from a decaying body was so repugnant that Mike had to put Vicks up his nose in order to withstand its permeating stench. The murder of a child was disconcerting, but a detective must ignore his feelings. Feigned insensitivity must be established in order to maintain professional composure. Keeping an open mind was necessary so that one did not become both judge and jury. Watching a medical examiner removing body organs required a strong stomach. Insidious nightmares did not allow him to forget all the gore.

The job could also be frustrating. Still to this day, the scales of justice are monetarily tilted. The most heinous criminal, if rich, can hire an extraordinary lawyer to take any advantage offered by a flawed judicial system. A poor criminal must entrust justice to an appointed public defender who is usually new to the field of law. The victim's scale is also adversely affected. Perpetrators are quite often sentenced to a facility with central air-conditioning, color TV, educational classrooms and three square meals a day. Some convicts have even been allowed an enormous income from biographies and memoirs.

My diary sympathizes: *Convicts often serve less than their actual sentencing time because of overcrowded prisons and early release programs. Detectives find themselves wondering why true justice is so difficult to secure.*

The nature of the job makes an investigator susceptible to dependent alcoholism, unacceptable failure, severe depression and wretched divorce. If he falls victim to any of these, the nicely dressed detective receives no gratitude, no understanding and no respect.

Imagine. There are people seeking this job! To Mike, the gold is a prestigious reward. My thought? I'm very happy. Mike's promotion means that he will no longer be first man in. He's been injured too many times.

CHAPTER 34

New Responsibilities (1982)

For the next twelve years, Mike worked in the Crimes Against Persons Division as an investigator dressed in a suit and tie and driving a plainclothes car. He perfected a stylish wardrobe. One, a black shirt, white tie and Italian shoes got attention! When his peers told him that he looked like one the bad guys, Mike's witty rebuttal would be, "It helps to fit in." During night shifts, he and his black partner took on the more casual look of the TV *Miami Vice* team.

Mike was responsible for the investigation of homicides, sexual assaults and sensitive cases (political, internal affairs and police shootings). During this period, he also gave class lectures to police cadets.

Constant "callbacks" became a way of life. Since the department did not normally staff its "C Squad" (midnight to 8:00 AM) with detectives, Mike would often clock out at midnight, get into bed around 1:30 AM and be awakened at 2:00, 3:00 or 4:00 AM to return. I was the one who would be awakened by the telephone. Mike would be too exhausted to hear it. The lieutenant would first apologize for waking me, and I would respond, "We have to stop meeting like this." But once

I woke Mike, his adrenaline would start pumping and provide the energy needed to meet the new challenge. With each new homicide, it was standard procedure for a "lead team" (two detectives) to work a straight twenty-four hours or more in order to complete an initial investigation. The first twenty-four hours are the most important because witnesses and evidence could be quickly lost.

Since many detectives refused to work with a female partner, it was to Detective Mike that women were assigned tutelage. Through the years, all types of partners came and went—male and female, big and petite, astute and obtuse. One great partnership lasted five years. Mike and Clyde were a good combination. Mike (white) and Clyde (black) became so well-known by the street population that they were christened with street names. "Iceman" was bestowed upon Mike. (Having little knowledge of the lexicon, I can only speculate upon the derivation of his nickname. Perhaps "Iceman" referred to Mike's calmness under fire or maybe it referred to his record of success for solving homicides. If you "ice" (kill) someone, the "Iceman" will come for you.) No matter the reason, Mike took no offense. In fact, he showed his appreciation by having the logo sewn onto his athletic jacket.

Mike liked all kinds of people. He judged everyone upon individual merit. This attribute allowed him clarity of purpose. Good people deserved justice. Yet gray areas did appear. At times, someone would commit a crime for understandable reasons. At other times, people were capable of cruel, self-serving things. Sometimes it was hard to tell just who the bad guys were! Mike's salvation from such dilemmas was the knowledge that he did his best to discover the truth of any given situation. For the sake of the truth, Mike dedicated himself to being thorough. He had to be "in the right" whenever a warrant application was signed or an arrest was made. Never could he lose sight of his responsibility to the victim or for the accused. Mike never wanted to put an innocent person in jail.

Spousal life became more stressful. Our children were now sixteen and eighteen. Each had a driver's license and sought the independence desired at that age. This allowed me to have more time to share with Mike, but he had less. To cope with this phenomenon, I immersed myself with new responsibilities of my own. I continued to drive my school bus and keep my position as a union steward. I also became secretary of our local union. My diary refers to our disconcerting karma: *I fear from this point on, our lives will be separate yet parallel.*

CHAPTER 35

Dirty Business (1983)

This case rudely introduced the new year. Apparently, peace and goodwill were foreign concepts to the people involved. Detective Mike and Detective Pete did the primary investigation and made the first arrest in this disturbing case. Sometime later, another police team helped conclude it with a second arrest. None of the investigators involved had ever handled a case such as this. The exploitation of one's own child was incomprehensible!

Mike and Pete had just completed their four-to-midnight shift. They were currently unwinding at the local bar, affectionately named the "Scum Keg".

"Damn," Mike cursed as his beeper went off. He had wanted to socialize, enjoy a few beers and go home to his wife. Then he thought, *Oh well, at least they caught me before I got all the way home*. He really would have disliked retracing the slippery highway in order to return for this recall.

When the detectives responded to Hill Avenue, they discovered the resident of the second-floor apartment dead. The body of the forty-two-year-old man had sustained several gunshot wounds about his torso. (The medical examiner would later confirm wounds to the lungs, aorta, liver and stomach.)

By interviewing family members, investigators learned that they had a very definite theory about the murder. They believed the victim, Jack, was deliberately executed because of financial problems with his business partner. Mike and Pete continued their investigation by canvassing the apartment building. The next-door neighbor heard a familiar voice at the victim's door earlier in the evening. It was the voice of a young man who was often seen in the building.

The resident of the first-floor apartment directly below had been awakened just before midnight by loud noises. He then heard footsteps running down the staircase. The front door of the building slammed. He got out of bed and opened his apartment door but saw no one. He then went to a window where he could view the adjacent empty lot. There, on the next street, he saw a familiar car pulling away. It was a vehicle sometimes driven by the victim.

More information was obtained, which encouraged the detectives to seek out the son of the victim's business partner. Since both the suspect and his father had ties in another town, the detectives directed their search to that area and discovered that the accused had been at a friend's home twice that evening. The friend stated that the suspect had left at approximately 11:00 PM but had awakened him two hours later (1:00 AM). He had returned looking for his father.

A third town became involved when police were sent to the residence of the suspect's father. At his hotel, the desk clerk greeted the officers and answered their inquiries. She did not believe the son was in because he had just called his father on the lobby phone at 1:16 AM (a few minutes prior to the officers' arrival). Police confirmed the room number and went to speak with the suspect's father. He informed them that his son had borrowed his car to visit friends out of town. It was the same make and color of the car seen driving in the immediate area of the murder. One hour later, the suspect returned to the hotel in that same vehicle. Town police took him into custody and transported him back to the city where the crime had taken place.

The young man signed a waiver of his rights and gave a voluntary statement in which he declared that Jack, the victim, had made homosexual advances toward him. He stated that Jack had also sprayed him with mace. At that point the suspect said that he shot Jack, using Jack's own .45-caliber pistol. After the shooting, he drove to his father's residence. On the way there, he supposedly changed clothes in his car. He said that he discarded both the mace-sprayed clothing and the pistol in a wooded area. He described the location, which was just off the highway.

Before the suspect was removed from the interview room, his father was allowed to speak to him. When the father entered, the son proclaimed, "It's all your fault. Just keep your mouth shut, and don't say anything." Then the two went to a corner of the room to speak softly. (Detectives believed that the son was attempting to silence his father. Since his father did not know what he had told the police, the suspect probably did not want his father to voice any discrepancies.) Just how much of the boy's statement was true? Did they arrest the right man?

In order to verify the son's confession, Mike and Pete continued their investigation. It was determined that the clean clothing he wore at the interview was, in fact, the same clothing that he had been wearing when he visited his friend's house at 1:00 AM. The clothing worn at the time of the murder was apparently different, so the statement about discarding the clothing may have been true. Several wooded areas along the highway were searched, but neither the handgun nor any clothes were found. The young man had lied about their hiding place.

The victim's housekeeper, children and former girlfriend were adamant that Jack never kept a gun in his home. They also vehemently denied the suspect's aspersions about Jack's sexual preference. Conversely, they declared the homosexual in this incident was not Jack but the accused himself. Detectives made many inquires but could not uncover any information, which indicated the victim might have had homosexual tendencies. That portion of the young man's statement was also considered to be false. But why did he lie?

During the ongoing investigation, detectives spoke to numerous people. Some believed that the father was also involved. The father held his partner, the victim, responsible for his pending divorce. Allegedly, the victim, Jack, had encouraged the woman not only to file for divorce, but to place an injunction against her husband's shares in the business. The father was sure that the motive for such marriage counselling was for Jack's own benefit. (With the father/husband financially tied up, Jack would have full control over their two mutually-owned companies.)

Other witnesses made a reference to yet another sour business deal. The father had claimed the theft of several oriental rugs worth thousands of dollars. The insurance company had denied the claim! Mike and Pete obtained a copy of the denial letter. It confirmed that the claim had been denied because of "misrepresentations" made by the father. At first, it seemed that the father had been stealing from the victim; but then, upon closer examination of the crime scene photos, some of the described "stolen" carpeting was right there in the victim's home. Both partners were apparently in on the insurance fraud scheme.

Thirteen months after the murder, the son was still incarcerated while awaiting trial. His father reneged many promises to post bail. The young man finally decided that he had been duped. No longer was he going to provide mute protection for his father. The man cared not one whit for him. He asked his lawyer to speak to the prosecuting attorney and set up an interview. He was ready to give "state's evidence".

At this time, Mike and Pete were working on two other murder cases, so another team was instructed to report to the State Attorney. There, they were informed that the suspect was willing to be interviewed in the presence of his attorney. Before commencing the interview, the accused was once again advised of his rights, and he acknowledged his understanding of them. A court stenographer typed his story: A month before the murder, his father had talked to him about discrepancies in the account books of the mutually-owned businesses. Hindsight now made the son realize that he really did not know if this accusation was true or whether it was just an excuse concocted to get rid of Jack. His father had also used another tactic. He brought up his son's own indebtedness. The young man owed his father three thousand dollars. His father promised this debt would be wiped out if his son agreed to help kill the business partner. He disclosed that his father's final lure was a promised partnership in the business. Allegedly, his father had told him, "Jack's death would be in both our best interests."

The son explained that his father wanted full control over both lucrative enterprises. This was because they were cash businesses, which allowed the owners to skim one-half the profits from the top before reporting any income to the IRS. Since Jack controlled the account books for both businesses, the father was not sure if he was getting his equal share of the stolen money. Even if he was, he did not like being totally dependent on Jack for the continuation of his illegal profits. He needed Jack eliminated so that he could control the books himself. Once in control, he would implement another plan. He would gain full ownership of the better company by squeezing Jack's widow out. His father planned to pay her only Jack's official salary recorded in the ledger, and she would not be able to do anything about the four-hundred-dollar weekly shortage. This would put her in such a bind that she would either agree to leave both businesses or at least trade her half of the better business for his half of the lesser business. He expected the trade to appeal to her because it would allow her to run the second business by herself in any manner she chose (legally or illegally).

The suspect told the police that his father had purchased the gun from the friend whose house he had twice visited on the night of the murder. He added that the man knew about the planned execution. The son had accompanied his father to the friend's home at an earlier date when a .45-caliber pistol, a clip and a box of cartridges had been delivered. That type of murder weapon had already been confirmed by previously secured evidence. A police evidentiary technician had examined seven .45-caliber spent cartridges taken from Jack's apartment. He also examined five .45-caliber copper-coated bullets that had been retrieved from Jack's body. The technician's report stated that each bullet had been fired from the same gun, thus verifying the murder was committed by one gun only (probably one man).

The young man continued, "During the next few weeks, my father became impatient and repeatedly encouraged me to kill Jack." His father constantly reminded him that it was the only way he could ever "square himself". At first, these detectives believed this remark referred to his three-thousand-dollar debt. But after consulting with the original investigating team (Mike and Pete), they understood that it meant much more! By committing murder, the son could prove himself to be **a man**. This was very important. Because of the son's homosexual tendencies, he never received the unconditional love he sought from his father.

Plans had been arranged long ago. His father had furnished him with information about the victim's car so that he could tell when Jack was home. He also told his son what approach route to use before entering the victim's home. His father had even arranged his own alibi by making sure he would be at the home of the gun supplying friend whenever the murder took place. He instructed his son to go straight to the alibi home after the murder, assuring him that he would be there waiting for him. This information confirmed *why* the murder took place. The father wanted it done!

Their next question was *how*? The son replied that his father gave him his reliable car in which he drove around for some time before stopping at a bar for a couple of drinks. He eventually made his way to the city and stayed at another bar until 11:30 PM. He then drove to the victim's neighborhood and parked the car one street away. He followed instructions to conceal himself by walking through the corridor of a building which led out to Hill Avenue. When Jack answered the door, the handgun was tucked in the young man's belt. He declared, "It was real hard to work up the nerve to kill him." Instead of drawing the gun, he asked Jack if he could stay the night. Jack replied, "Sorry, I've got some girls coming over, so you'll have to leave." But Jack did give him money for a motel. The accused then left the apartment but only went as far as the front steps. He told the detectives that he waited there while deciding that he just could not go back to face his father with the news that he did not do it. He returned and was admitted to Jack's apartment under the false pretense that he had left his wallet. Once inside he fumbled around looking for it. As Jack was talking on the telephone, he drew out the gun and shot him four or five times. (The person on the other end of the telephone was located, and she confirmed hearing the son's voice and the shots.) He then ran from the apartment, taking the gun with him.

Instead of driving directly to the alibi house, he first headed to his father's residence to change his bloody clothes. On the way, he exited the highway and dropped the gun into a sewer on Town Road. He entered his father's empty residence via the side entrance, changed his clothes (dark-navy-blue Air Force jacket with fur collar, dark-blue sweater, white shirt), placed them into a trash bag and then left the hotel. While in route to the friend's house, he deposited the bag of clothes into an industrial dumpster. By the time he arrived at the friend's home, his father had given up waiting for him. He was no longer there. When the friend asked how it went, his reply was, "Okay...I guess." He used his friend's phone to call his father. When his father got on the line, his son just said, "It happened." Shortly after, he departed from the friend's home and once again traveled to his father's hotel, where he was subsequently taken into custody.

The next day, the detectives once again interviewed the accused in the presence of his attorney. They asked him to elaborate on financial matters. When asked the dollar amounts of the two businesses, the son informed the detectives that one was worth approximately $76,000 while the other was worth $86,000. He also stated that his debts to his father consisted of a $2,000 college loan and the rest of the money was incurred using his father's charge card. His promised reward of stock shares was to be one-half of his father's shares in both companies.

He clarified other information as well. When asked about the gun, he knew only that someone named Jim had delivered it to the friend, who then sold it to his father. He verified that on the day of the delivery, his father had loaded it and given it to him to keep in his possession. When asked if any prior plans had been made should anything go wrong, he affirmed, "If anything went wrong, I was supposed to go to a family friend in Florida."

The detectives asked the suspect if he would further cooperate by making two phone calls: one to the gun supplying friend and the other to his father. (The detectives hoped that each man would make self-incriminating statements.) When the young man spoke to the friend, he told him that the police had found the gun. The friend replied, "I don't know anything about that. Call your father." (No luck there.) His father was surprised to hear from him. He first asked if his son was out on bond, then continued his conversation with speculation about the amount of time his son might get if he were convicted. His boy informed him that he had just called the friend and told him that the police had found the gun. The father was startled and proclaimed, "You shouldn't have told him anything. Shut your fucking mouth! Why did you tell him anything? You're dead and so is he because he'll tell Jim [the gun dealer]! You're both dead!"

Based on that conversation, detectives were assured that the father did plot to murder his business partner, and that he did hire his son to do the killing. Payment was by virtue of eliminating his son's $3,000 debt and promising him a business partnership. The affiants (detectives) requested a warrant for the father, charging him with Capital Felony Murder.

Diary entry: *This father's abusive parenting ruined his son's life! The twenty-two-year-old, college graduate was sentenced to thirty years in prison. His deplorable father (age forty-nine) was sentenced to life.*

CHAPTER 36

Acquittal (1983)

"City Man Says Police Tried to Frame Him." Vern is continuing his mantra of persecution. Vern (now forty-two years old) was on the front page of the newspaper, but this story was old news. Once again, he was claiming police harassment. The article explained that Vern was allegedly involved in a double shooting back in October 1981. At that time, he stood accused of both murder and an assault, which had transpired because of a drug deal gone sour. By December, Vern had been arraigned and subsequently indicted by an eighteen-member grand jury and bound for trial. Now it was March 1983. A twelve-member superior court jury, having heard evidence for over a week, deliberated only two hours before **acquitting** him!

Vern and his defense attorney claimed, "The charges were a frame-up by police who have had a vendetta against the defendant since 1971 when Vern assaulted a policeman with his car." Incredible! Vern's lawyer was using Mike's injury as a defense!

Police assured the court that the case was initiated only because a witness had reported the incident. The witness had relayed, "Two victims were walking toward the Destiny Lounge about 10:15 PM when a gunman opened fire on them." The deceased was found around the corner from the lounge, and the other wounded victim was found on Matthew Street.

The state's case was damaged by two things:

1. At the last minute, their key witness, the man who saw the shooting, refused to testify. (Sound familiar?)
2. The surviving victim was now serving a sentence himself in a state prison for an unrelated case. Therefore, the jury questioned his credibility.

Vern's attorney exposed both victims as drug dealers and declared the survivor to be a notorious felon. He proclaimed the state should have been wary of using him as their key witness. (The felon only became the key witness after the man who had reported the crime would not testify.) The defense attorney declared that he had based his stand on good alibi witnesses (never in short supply). He reminded the jury that Vern openly acknowledged that he **once** was a drug dealer and had been involved in other illegal activities. Vern's auto business on Main Street was presented as proof that he was now an honest business man.

The defense attorney's allegation against the police was based upon the fact that it had taken police nine days to get the accusing statement from the assaulted victim. He declared, "This fact leads me to believe that police manipulated this guy." (The delay was due to the survivor's very poor medical condition.)

While awaiting trial, Vern spent five and a half months in jail before he was able to post a $50,000 bond. His lawyer proclaimed, "The time spent in jail is something my innocent client can never recover."

My diary notes an opposite view: *A few months in jail is all the punishment this criminal will receive for these felonies. I'm afraid "payback" may never come due. This bad penny continues to turn heads-up.*

Meanwhile, Mike's **bad** luck continued. In November 1983, his weak right ankle just slipped off the first step in the police station stairwell. The dress shoes that Mike started wearing when he became a detective would have to be replaced by supportive cowboy boots.

CHAPTER 37

Roll Reversal (1983)

For a child who hated grammar school, Lonny certainly surprised us. He wanted to go to college, major in business and become a Certified Public Accountant. Scholastic scores granted him acceptance into three private colleges. Having a high school sweetheart had a lot to do with his school of choice. Lisa had one more year of high school, so Lonny chose to commute to a nearby college. This would give them one more year together before she entered college. But she would not be going far either. She chose to study special education in an adjoining state. Both promised alternating weekend visits.

Lonny played college hockey (I was the team's bus driver). He earned good grades, which kept him on the Dean's List. Surprisingly, one of his most difficult courses was "Expository Writing". Because he knew of my love for writing, he one day asked, "Hey, Mom, can you take a look at this?" That was it. I was hooked. I became a student again—my dining room a classroom. Lonny shared his notes, his books and his ideas. We spent hours together editing his papers. We joked. We lamented. We tossed around crazy ideas. We traded philosophies...**We communicated.**

Working together was fun. Lonny's stories gave me wonderful insight into this maturing young man—my son. On occasion, he would find some small way to let me know that he appreciated my help. In my scrapbook, there is a preserved Mother's Day card. On the front is a sketch of a young mother sitting at a kitchen table. Her left arm is securing a small unhappy child in her lap. With an ink pen in her right hand and a determined expression on her face, she has managed to write three lines. Her facial expression depicts concentration greater than that required for a grocery list. The puppy chewing on the toe of her slipper is being completely ignored. Surely the lines are the beginning of a new idea. The print reads:

> *Dear Mom,*
>   *Now I know there's more to being a mother than, cooking, cleaning, sewing, teaching, learning, labor, toil, exhaustion **and English papers**.* (His insertion was made correctly.)

The inside read:

> *That's just the fun part!*

It was apparent that Lonny had remembered the story I had told him about my first college English course. Because of Lonny's late arrival, I had missed the first class that semester but did manage to begin with the second class. Lonny was only one week old when Mike began babysitting. I entered the classroom carrying a cushion. It was necessary if I was going to sit through an entire lecture. But that was not even the hard part! Finishing weekly assignments was a real challenge. Lonny was a colicky baby and in constant need of my left shoulder. I did not realize how beneficial that English class would be for both me and my baby. I guess Lonny was now glad that I completed it.

My children seemed to have reversed rolls. The grades of Lori, our honor roll student, began slipping. Now a high school junior, she wanted to be taken out of accelerated classes, so I made an appointment to see her guidance counselor. He told me that Lori was becoming quite a socialite. He felt that she preferred free time for friends rather than to study. He said that allowing her easier classes would just play into her hands. He advised, "Don't let her become lazy. She has a high IQ."

On the drive home, I considered his advice. I thought, *He is a professional educator. He should know what he's talking about. Maybe I'm inclined to be too easy.* Mike and I decided to maintain Lori's present placement. What a mistake! I should have followed my own instincts. Lori's next report card was much less satisfactory. I called the counselor again. He declared, "She can't get good grades when she misses so much school."

Incredulously I replied, "What do you mean?" Since her father had been dropping her off every morning, I hadn't bothered to check the attendance portion of her report card. But there in front of me was the proof. Apparently, she had been walking in the front door, only to walk out the back!

Disillusioned, I scrawled, *Now it is Lori's turn to drive me nuts. Is she acting like this to get her father's attention? Could she be trying to embarrass him? A cop's child is expected to be perfect! How can I help when I do not understand what is happening?* **How do I get her to communicate?**

CHAPTER 38

Frozen Evidence (1984)

It was a beautiful spring day! The vivid blue sky embraced a couple of white cotton-puff clouds. The air was moderately warm and pleasantly dry, and its slight breeze gently wafted the scent of newly mowed grass. It was the kind of day that caused one to stand still for just one minute, take a deep breath and feel good to be alive. It should not have been a day for a child to die.

Three days earlier: The phone rang at the police department. The voice of a tired ER doctor was calling to report a child abuse case. This time, a baby appeared to have been shaken and strangled!

Detectives Mike and Dan responded to the hospital. They first spoke with two doctors and then went to view the little boy being sustained on life support. The infant was technically listed as critical. Little Jay had bruises on his neck, face, right shoulder and back. The detectives took photos and obtained those already taken by the hospital staff.

Both young parents were interviewed separately, but each investigator began his interview with these same questions:

1. Has the baby had any previous injuries?

2. Has another family member, or any other person, recently been in contact with the child?

Mom and Dad responded that there had been no previous injury and that they were the only ones in contact with the child for the past week.

After the interviews, the detectives left the distraught parents and returned to the station to review the doctor's written reports. From experience, Mike knew it to be unusual for a doctor to willingly verify child abuse with a written statement. Why? Perhaps too many variables were possible, and the doctors did not want to waste precious time in a court of law. But this time the detectives had **two** doctors who were willing to substantiate child abuse! Among the list of injuries, Dr. M listed ecchymosis (multiple bruises) on the chin and neck.

Later, Mike and Dan located the unwed couple and requested that they voluntarily give sworn statements. Agreeing, they were transported back to headquarters in an unmarked unit with no mechanical restraints (handcuffs or locked doors). They were advised of their rights and documented their understanding by signing a waiver form. It was arranged for a female detective to take the mother's statement while Mike took the father's. The young man relayed the following: He was Jay's father. Although he resided in the same building as the mother and his son, he had his own apartment. However, he often stayed with them. Around midnight, he was babysitting in his girlfriend's apartment when he started to play with his son. He described tossing the child into the air several times. Then he tripped on a rug, which caused him to miss catching Jay. During the baby's decent, his chin struck the father's forehead. The baby's neck then struck the crib before finally landing on the floor. The father's portrayal could explain the many bruises.

Was this incident just an unfortunate accident because of a stupid act?

The mother's statement affirmed that when she arrived, her boyfriend was upset. He told her about playing with the baby and that Jay's chin had hit his forehead. He said that he was sorry. Since all was now quiet, she did not immediately check on the baby. She assumed her boyfriend had put Jay to bed for the night. Approximately fifteen minutes later, she viewed Jay asleep but did notice a red mark on his chin. Mother and father went to bed. The baby's crib was in the same bedroom, and all slept through the night. They checked on Jay often that next day. On Sunday, the baby became fussy but did nurse without any problem. He was awake most of the day. On Monday, Jay woke up at 8:00 AM, at which time his mother changed and nursed him before going back to sleep. She awoke about 10:00 AM to the baby's fussing. Jay was whitish-blue in color. She stated that his color improved after she gave him mouth-to-mouth, but he was still having difficulty breathing. She left him in the middle of her bed and went running to the father's apartment for help. Both ran back to her place where the father began pressing on Jay's chest and stomach area. She grabbed a blanket to wrap the baby and told her boyfriend they had to get Jay to the hospital. There, medical personnel were still caring for her baby when the two police detectives approached them. She admitted, "I told him to say nothing about dropping the baby."

On the second day of the investigation, Mike checked on the baby's condition. The doctor informed him that nothing else could be done. The baby would not survive. Both Mike and the doctor needed time. Mike wanted to know who was responsible. The doctor wanted to contact the organ donor network. Together, they agreed that the parents would not be told until one more test was completed.

Mike telephoned the mother and asked if she would come to the police station to discuss some important information. (To ascertain the truth, a detective must often bluff. If she believed that Mike had more information than he really did, she may decide to change her original statement.) Mike told the mother that he really knew Jay had been shaken because the whites of his eyes were pink with blood when he arrived at the ER. (This was true, but other things could also cause this same condition.)

Mike went on to confide that he was also a parent, and he knew from experience just how difficult it was. He understood about being tired all the time from night feedings and crying. She shared the fact, "My baby cries all the time for nothing." She said, "The constant crying got on his nerves, so he shook Jay to shut him up."

On the third day of the investigation (4:10 PM), a Chicago retrieval team was on call. The hospital social worker informed the detectives that Jay was now considered brain dead. She was going to inform the parents. At 7:30 PM, Dr. K counseled the young couple about withdrawing the life-sustaining apparatus from the infant. He explained that this would constitute the death of their child and asked them about donating the baby's organs. At 8:00 PM, a joint decision was made. At 8:15 PM, Jay was pronounced dead. His short life had only lasted three months and four days.

Mike and Dan were saddened by the baby's death, and both felt sorry for the distressed parents. Since their investigation had uncovered no evidence of previous abuse (no medical records and no witnesses), they felt this was just an unfortunate tragedy. Even so, a child had died, and standard procedure dictated that the detectives execute a manslaughter warrant for the father.

The next day, Mike and an evidentiary detective attended the infant's autopsy. A state medical examiner found injuries along Jay's spinal column, which appeared to have occurred earlier than those injuries that had caused his death. The doctor pointed out each injury and explained that each had reached a different degree of healing. This indicated that Jay had been hurt on several occasions. Mike's rage exploded, "Goddamn it!" He was angry that Jay had suffered such brutality, and he was angry at himself for being duped into giving the father the benefit of a doubt. But his anger was useful, for it sustained him throughout the rest of the autopsy. With gritted teeth and clenched fists, he watched the doctor methodically remove Jay's tiny spinal cord. It would be frozen so that it could be later produced as evidence. It would tell what Jay could not.

Questions remained. Which parent was inflicting injury? Were both responsible? Both had lied! There were no medical records indicating treatment for past injuries; therefore, neither parent sought treatment for their son. Even if Jay's mother was not directly responsible for his injures, she certainly had to know what was happening! Why did she not stop it? The postmortem statement labeled Jay's death "Homicide due to closed head trauma, with subdural hemorrhage, with survival in coma for two days."

Mike's investigation continued. He now knew that Jay's death was no accident, and he relished upgrading the charge from manslaughter to murder. A search warrant secured a blue baby sleeper, baby blankets, one pair of men's black ski pants, one women's multicolored sweater, many pieces of bloodstained tissues and medical reports. More interviews were performed, and more contacts were made. One doctor gave additional information: While caring for Jay, she had also found signs of a broken ankle, which were confirmed by x-ray.

The investigation came to an end when Mike served a murder warrant on the father, who responded, "I only hit Jay to discipline him when he cried for no reason."

Hearing this, Mike's jaw tightened as he hissed his controlled reply, "When a baby cries, there *is* a reason!"

Jay's mother was also charged. She was arrested for manslaughter because she did not protect her child, and she continued to leave him at risk. I thought neighboring tenants should have been charged as accessories. The bold scrawl in my diary demonstrates my anger with such people: *They certainly heard the child's excruciating screams when he was being abused, but because they chose not to become involved, Jay's torture continued! Mike feels angry and frustrated. Jay didn't have to die!*

For the next several nights, I was awakened by Mike's tossing and turning. He was plagued with vivid memories: the beauty of Jay's fragile innocence as he slept, and the overwhelming ugliness of Jay's spinal cord being excised.

Diary: *It is no wonder that cops struggle with cynicism and depression. Too many bright sunny days become instantly overcast.*

CHAPTER 39

Vern versus the CITY Et Al.
(1984 Federal Civil Rights Case)

A distraught diary entry states: *Mike has once again been accused of being a bad guy. This time it is serious! He has been named as a defendant in a federal case. Who made the allegations? Vern, the returning bad penny. He has accused not only Mike, but named six other police officers, unknown officers and the city. All are alleged to have violated his civil rights.* The plaintiff's lawyer had requested that each individually named officer answer, under oath, pages of interrogatories pertaining to this case. Rule 33 of Federal Rules of Civil Procedure required answers within thirty days. Since the initial contact with the city's lawyer, the plaintiff had withdrawn fourteen questions, leaving thirty interrogatories (ten pages) to be answered!

While all parties were named in the United States District Court summons, Officer Mike was specifically mentioned in the following sections:

- No. 6: Officer Michael has threatened and harassed the plaintiff without just or proper cause.

- No. 11: During 1971 the plaintiff was stopped by Officer Michael for an alleged motor violation. The plaintiff was ordered out of his motor vehicle and as he nervously exited the car it accidentally rolled forward and/or somehow engaged its gears and the car, while moving forward, did harmlessly and, without injury, strike the officer. It is believed that the officer did indicate this action to other officers and did represent it as an intentional act by the plaintiff with the intent to harm the officer; that thereafter, the police officers of the city did have an intent to damage or harm or accuse the plaintiff of various illegal or unlawful actions in order to get him into trouble.
- No. 14. c.: In September 1979, defendant Michael, threatened and harassed the plaintiff in numerous ways at both his home and his place of business. Subsequently, this officer arrested the plaintiff without a warrant and without legal ground or probable cause.

The plaintiff's lawyer, Juris…, had also requested the city produce the following:

1. Any documents concerning every arrest and transportation of the plaintiff from 1971 to 1982.
   a. Statements or interviews of witnesses, the plaintiff, police officers, medical personnel or other persons regarding these incidents.
   b. All chronologies prepared by any police officer involved in any incident with the plaintiff.
   c. All police reports prepared as a result of every arrest, detention or transportation of the plaintiff;

all investigations material of the police department or of the prosecuting authority after 1971.

d. All incident reports concerning every arrest of the plaintiff and/or search of his person, home and/or business.

e. All complaints filed against the plaintiff as a result of the arrest.

2. All witnesses, photographs, physical objects, diagrams or other documents of any party in this case.

3. All documents relating to any administrative com-plaints against the defendants (officers) from 1971 to 1982 including, but not limited to, violations of personnel regulations and violations of internal procedures.

4. All performance evaluations and any other similar documents concerning each defendant from the date of his appointment as a city officer to the present.

5. All documents regarding any applications for criminal complaints against the defendants (officers) for alleged misconduct.

6. All annual reports, summaries or other such similar documents regarding the functioning of the Internal Affairs Division of the Police Department from 1971 to 1982.

Other policemen were named for wrongful arrests.

- When Vern was arrested for rape, the case never went to trial because the victim disappeared.

- When he was arrested for murder, one eye witness refused to testify, and the other victim/witness was a criminal, so the jury rendered a "Not Guilty" verdict.

The charge for wounding the drug dealer in that same incident was never pursued because the prosecutor foresaw a similar outcome.

The summons concludes: The plaintiff requests compensatory and punitive damages for the wrongful arrests, the malicious prosecution of charges against the plaintiff, the intentional infliction of emotional distress, the loss of reputation and economical loss in the amount of **$5,000,000**.

Mike's own attorney immediately sought and was granted a lien on any reward that may be won by the plaintiff. Should Vern win any portion of this federal suit against other officers or the city, the related damages would have to be used to fulfill Vern's responsibility to Mike. It would be an extraordinary means by which to finally collect damages from Vern! Mike knew he was innocent of any wrongdoing, but if the outcome of the other counts went in Vern's favor, Mike would reap the reward. No matter the outcome, Vern was not going to win because he would either lose the case or lose his winnings! My diary states: *Even if Mike receives no money from this ridiculous situation, being able to destroy Vern's expectation of a windfall has been a small victory for us. Will skirmishes with this lowlife ever cease?*

(In 1985, a federal judge ruled against the plaintiff on all counts. All defendants were deemed innocent; to Mike, he directed this statement, "Officer Michael, I'm sorry you will receive no monetary reward.")

CHAPTER 40

Arrogance or Diligence? (1984)

The responsibility for an investigation lay squarely upon the shoulders of a two-person "lead team". So when Mike and a partner were designated to lead, they took total control of a crime scene. Mike was demanding, exacting and relentless. Once, he even asked his supervisor to leave an apartment because it had not yet been properly processed. Detectives from the Evidentiary Service Unit could attest to Mike's reputation for thoroughness. These detectives received instructions as to what was to be secured, collected and processed. Detective Mike always wanted everything! He would preach, "You can always throw away what you don't need, but you can never go back to get it. Even if you could, it would be considered tainted." When disgruntled processing detectives or supervisors complained about excessive evidence bags or the cost of film, Mike would quip, "I need a lot of evidence to justify all the overtime I'm going to be putting on everyone's time cards." (His diligence was not always appreciated!) Eventually, detectives from evidentiary services learned to ask who the lead investigator was. If it was Mike, they automatically took along added supplies.

Once a harried peer complained to Mike that he was an arrogant S.O.B. Without penance, Mike absolved himself with this mordant response, "You can be arrogant if you're right!" Even the occasionally miffed coworkers never refused to work with him because there was opportunity for learning, potential for clearance and possibilities for overtime.

He expected professionalism from everyone. In fact, he assured it by making himself aware of every detail in a case. Accountability was a serious matter. He would often remind, "If I'm going to be the one testifying under oath, on the hot seat (witness stand), I'm going to make damn sure that everything is done right." Management, of course, always wanted quick investigations and immediate arrests. Most were interested in producing favorable clerical statistics and acquiring excellent press releases. But Mike remained adamant. "There is a time to hurry up and a time to slow down." He was not just interested in making arrests. He was determined to build sound cases for prosecution. Such diligence rewarded Mike with an outstanding record. (When Mike was the lead investigator, cases culminated with convictions.)

To assure that he was right, Mike reviewed each solved case in an effort to exonerate the accused. If he could not do so, he remained content with the arrest. Mike believed, "Both the victim and the accused deserved justice." He would never forget being mistreated by cops when he was a teenager wrongly accused of stealing tires.

My thought: *I believe Mike's character derives from equal portions of diligence and arrogance. Should arrogance begin to dominate, I interject a reminder, "Be nice."*

CHAPTER 41

From Princess to Queen (1984)

My cop was a prince who enjoyed his princess. But now he was wondering just how his chosen lady had changed from the lovely maiden who needed his protection to a stalwart matron who resisted his authority! My transformation began a long time ago, but its onset had gone unnoticed.

Little things happened. A snowstorm caused Mike to work overtime, and a parking ban was in effect long before his arrival. When I got home from work, snowplows had already come by. It was up to me to open the driveway and get my car off the street. So I took a snow shovel in hand and began to dig. It took me an hour to make an opening through the barricade, which several snowplows had so meticulously constructed. The next day, I asked Mike to show me how to start the snow blower. What happened to the damsel in distress?

At first, Mike worked a lot of extra hours due to monetary necessity. (It took overtime to match his once-lucrative income.) Then personal necessity took over. He was seduced by the excitement and the challenge. While he was out crusading, I learned to reign over Camelot. It was not a glorious task!

When Mike's knee injury exempted him from ladders, I painted the outside of the house. (That took me an entire summer.) While Mike was in court, the sewer backed up, and I had to take care of it. Since plunging did not work, five telephone calls finally found a plumber who would render immediate service. I even began to balance our check book! I became quite proficient, very self-reliant and **too** independent. I began to make family decisions on my own. (Most of the time, Mike was happy to relinquish them to me.)

The princess became a queen while the prince was becoming a king. Now, she and he had to learn how to rule jointly. Neither must be too proud, for two self-important, uncompromising people could only produce discord. My diary notes: *Occasionally I solicit amiability by resurrecting the princess. But it is difficult to abdicate.*

CHAPTER 42

Dogs Hinder—Fish Help (1984)

It was in September when detectives Mike and Dell were sent to the waterfront. At 6:30 PM, the body of an adult male had been found under some bushes near the dock. It appeared to be a homicide because someone had tried to cover the body with a large sheet of brown wrapping paper. One bloody hand was left exposed. Upon Mike's arrival, he called the fire department and asked them to provide much-needed lighting. Since the crime scene was a large open place, he procured a few overtime patrolmen from the Field Service Division to secure the area. Then he summoned two evidentiary detectives to come and process the scene.

While awaiting the medical examiner, Mike and Dell questioned a nearby fisherman. When he was asked if he had seen anyone in the area, he described a light-skinned black male with green eyes. Upon his arrival, this man had flagged him down and asked for help. He had explained that his girlfriend had driven the car off the road and had got stuck in the mud. But when John (the fisherman) went to push the blue and white Cadillac out, there was no female present. As he and the stranger tried to jack the car up, John noticed blood spattered on the left rear fender where its chrome paneling was coming off. Because the car would not budge, the stranger summoned another white male, who was now parking his green pickup truck on top of the hill close to the dock. When he came down to help, John got into the car to steer as the others pushed from the front. While inside, John noticed its blue interior and a clear plastic bag sitting in the passenger seat. It was filled with water and two live goldfish. After freeing the car, John returned to fishing.

When the evidentiary detectives arrived, Mike asked one officer to make casts of both the sneaker prints and the tire tracks. The other stymied detective was asked to retrieve the bag of goldfish now laying a short distance down the road. At first this request only received some good-natured ribbing. It took Mike's unflappable persistence to produce compliance by the disgruntled detective.

No doubt the medical examiner took the time to have her dinner before coming to the scene. She finally arrived at 8:05 PM with two unleashed bodyguards. Her large Dobermans reached the body first and immediately decimated the brown paper with urine. Talk about tainted evidence! Mike's disgust was palpable. "Son of a bitch!" (The pun was intended.) He had planned to secure the paper as evidence so that a fuming process could be done, which would disclose latent prints. Now, that was not possible. Mike was still furious as the "bimbo doc" pronounced, "Death seems to have been caused by several blows to the head, probably from a blunt instrument." (The severity of the head wounds and the information about the bloody car fender made that perfectly obvious.) She also advised, "The depressions in the victim's chest suggest he's been kicked." (The footprints had already been cast.) After turning the body over, she searched his pockets but found no wallet or any other form of identification.

The detectives did not even know who he was, never mind who had killed him!

The next morning, Mike and Dell set out to canvas every pet store, including those in surrounding communities. They queried many salespeople, "Have you recently sold two goldfish to this man?" (The one that lay dead in their Polaroid picture.) Finally, one store owner recognized the victim. He identified Allen as a regular customer who had just purchased fish the day before. Fortunately, his purchase had been charged. The voucher supplied Allen's address, but before going to a family with such tragic news, Mike sought one more verification. He contacted the motor vehicle department. They verified that the owner of the goldfish was also the owner of a car matching the make and color described by the fisherman, John. Now Mike felt confident that he was going to the right family with the bad news.

When he and his partner arrived at the victim's home, they noticed no such car. Before knocking on the door, Mike took a deep breath. He really hated this part of his job, but a family member would have to officially identify Allen's body. Before leaving for the morgue, he verified the fact that Allen's car was missing and arranged to have a description of the stolen vehicle broadcast throughout the state.

Mike's department was contacted by police thirty-five miles away. The officer did not yet know that the Cadillac was in his town. He was merely inquiring about a possible assault being perpetrated upon a party only known by his first name, Allen. He was asking because hospital personnel in his town had called him about a man whom they had admitted into their detoxification center. Their patient had been sputtering about badly hurting someone and then taking his Cadillac. Even though the patient had threatened to kill anyone who might notify the police, his threats were ignored because a person may be somewhere injured and requiring help. Having no knowledge of an assault in his own town, the officer had decided to check with police in the patient's hometown. After speaking to Mike, he went to the hospital and found the car in the private parking lot. He verified the Cadillac to be the same one Mike was looking for.

When city police responded to the suburban town, they learned that the accused had received a motor vehicle violation while driving the victim's Cadillac. It was dated the very same day as the victim's death. The motor vehicle stop had been made before the stolen broadcast had gone out, so the driver had been allowed to go on his way. Even so, this evidence was extremely important because it placed the accused in the stolen car, which proved the suspect was a thief. Town police could now arrest the suspect for second-degree larceny and impound the car. After that booking procedure, city detectives would have a picture of the suspect. It was needed to construct a photo array, which would be used to continue their murder investigation. The incarceration of the suspect also assured that his clothes would be secured, thus remaining admissible evidence. Mike would obtain them with a warrant. The sneakers, sweatshirt and blue jeans worn at the time of his larceny arrest appeared to be bloodstained.

Before questioning him about the murder, city detectives once again read him his rights. The accused stated that he understood his rights and went on to tell the police that he had received the car from a friend. He first declared that he did not know the man's name because they had just met. Then he changed his story, stating he joined Allen in the city and had driven around for a couple of days. He mentioned being stuck in some mud but was helped by two white guys.

The fisherman identified the suspect's picture from the photo array. He was quite sure that TD was the person who had asked him for help. John was also shown a picture of the car. He was positive about its identification, pointing out the damage to the chrome molding. The forensic tests verified the blood on the suspect's clothing as the blood of the deceased. The affiants obtained and executed a murder warrant. Another warrant was issued for the victim's vehicle, still safely impounded in the other town.

Mike continued to investigate this case. He wanted to know the motive for this crime before the case went to trial. Since Mike had to notify the family of the arrest, he also used his visit to reinterview them. He was told that the family did not know the accused. The victim was retired. His hobby was his fish tank, and his habit was viewing old movies.

The victim often went to one specific theater. (Mike knew it to be a well-known gay pickup spot around which many robberies had been reported.) Mike and his partner interviewed employees and frequent patrons. They verified that both the deceased and the accused were regulars, but the accused was not gay. So why was he a regular customer? Did he go there seeking robbery victims? (Gays were considered "easy marks".) One person remembered seeing the two leave together on the day of the murder.

After the suspect's arrest, the robberies in that area ceased. It seemed Allen was murdered because he resisted being robbed by an addict.

Thank God Mike sought help from those goldfish.

CHAPTER 43

The Danger of Cash (March 1984–December 1984)

4:30 AM: I awakened to the telephone and quickly lifted its receiver before it could resound the second annoying ring. By now, I had become well accustomed to the routine, as was the caller. Lieutenant Joe no longer bothered to apologize for interrupting my sleep. He merely said, "Good morning." Then he waited for me to wake Mike.

A minute later, Joe heard a groggy "Hi." The next sound was a plaintive moan as Mike noticed the time on the bedside clock. Finally, he forced his tongue to ask a semiconscious question, "What's up?"

Joe answered, "We've had a shooting incident. It looks like a homicide."

Mike pushed himself up into a more wakeful position and asked, "Where?"

The lieutenant instructed him to respond directly to Oliver Street, where his partner would meet him.

To replace the phone, Mike had to reach over me. As he did so, he gave me a short, but tender kiss on the cheek. This one second in time would have to suffice as our quality time for the day. Since it took many hours to complete the initial portion of a new investigation, I knew that Mike probably would not be home until sometime the next day. Before rising, Mike better secured the covers around me and whispered, "Go back to sleep."

"Too late for that." I mourned, "My alarm's going to go off in a half hour." But I dosed until the aroma of coffee lured me from beneath the cozy comforter. Too soon, I would be outside in the cold scraping the March frost off the six mirrors strategically placed around the front of my seventy-one-passenger school bus.

At the same time, Mike would be arriving at his latest murder scene. There he would find a black male with an apparent gunshot wound behind his left ear. His body was lying on its right side in the grassy area west of the curb line. His trousers were pulled down to his knees, exposing his lower torso. Was this an execution? Was it a sex crime? It could be just a foiled robbery, because a hundred yards north was a Yellow Cab, parked with its door open and its motor running. The cab company was contacted, and they identified the victim as their operator. He was thirty-six years old.

A detective from evidentiary services arrived to process the established crime scene. Under Mike's direction, he took several photos and measurements. He made diagrams and collected several pieces of evidence, including samples of nearby blood droppings.

At 5:58 AM, the new medical examiner arrived to officially pronounce the victim dead. From the doctor's initial findings, he concurred the homicide appeared to be caused by a single gunshot wound to the head. At the "post", the doctor found a secondary head injury as well. The victim had also been struck by a blunt object. Had the victim put up a fight? Did anyone see the struggle?

The company supplied the cab's last known location. At a women's request, it had been sent to 104 Clover Avenue. After investigating the residence, it appeared that no one from that address had made the call. (Anyone could have used their address as a pickup point.) Every explored avenue came to a dead end. It was most probably a random robbery that had turned into a murder. Unfortunately, random crimes were always difficult to solve.

Seven months later, the case was still unsolved when Mike and his partner went to a regular staff meeting. These weekly meetings were attended by all the detectives within the division. They were designed to update everyone. Each detective found out the following:

1. What was going on throughout the city.
2. Who oversaw each investigation.
3. How much progress was made.
4. Which criminals were involved.
5. Where help was needed.

Mike became very attentive as he listened to a report by another detective. The MO (modus operandi) in his solved robbery case sounded familiar. A cabdriver had been robbed at gunpoint by his fare who had been picked up on Field Street. Bingo! That street was in the same immediate area where Mike's murdered cabdriver had picked up his last fare.

Also, at this meeting was another detective who relayed that a woman had once spoken to him about the murder. At the time, she had told the officer that her son was very upset about the cabdriver's death. Since grasping at straws was a common practice, Mike and his partner would make sure to speak to her. But first, he wanted to interview the two suspects while both were still in custody—awaiting a bail hearing for the solved robbery.

A female had been arrested for the current robbery. Also arrested was her brother, Gary. Mike interviewed both separately. He pressed each for information about the March homicide and told each of them that their method of operation implicated them in that homicide. (In both cases, a female had ordered a cab to the same area, and the driver was robbed by his fare.) Finding out they had become suspects in Mike's murder case made both siblings extremely nervous. Both remained adamant that they had nothing to do with it. It was unfortunate for Mike that these young adults were brother and sister because they remained loyally silent. Before ending each interview, Mike assured, "You **are** going down for the Oliver Street murder." This proved to be a mistake; for once forewarned, they did everything in their power to come up with bail money. Since Mike had no concrete evidence for a murder charge, the bond was minimally set for a mere robbery. Both were released and disappeared.

Mike and Danny staunchly continued the search for evidence that would prove their involvement in the homicide. They went to the mother, who had been discussed at the staff meeting, and she gave them the name of another woman with whom she had discussed the murder. She also informed the detectives that she expected the $20,000 reward, which the District Attorney was now offering for an arrest and conviction. Before leaving her home, the detectives approached her son. The nervous young man had **too much** information! His knowledge of details, which had been carefully kept secret, incriminated him.

Mike so informed the young man. To the mother's surprise, her own son was now a suspect!

Her boy admitted that he knew the identity of the murderer but sought to use the information to save his own skin. He offered to trade his knowledge to the state prosecutor. In return, he wanted to be assured that he would receive a light sentence. Mike and Danny reviewed the case with a state prosecutor. Because this murder would probably never be solved without this young man's input, the attorney agreed to deal.

In November, the detectives took the informant's sworn statement. Within those five pages, he revealed his part in the planning and execution of several armed robberies. All were perpetrated by the same people: himself, another man, Gary and his sister. He gave names and specified which robberies had originated from the woman's residence. He also said that Gary always carried a handgun, while he, himself, only carried a large wrench. (Another witness would eventually say that this informer carried a shotgun as well as the wrench on the night of the murder.)

Also located was the female who had conversed with the mother about the murder. She recalled that conversation and restated it to the officers: "I had housed a friend (another of Gary's sisters) for a couple of nights before she left for Florida. While at my house, she told me that her brother had murdered a cabdriver." Detectives vigorously searched for the accused but were unable to find Gary anywhere in the state. He was eventually located in Florida. Because Gary had not returned to court for the robbery charge, he had broken his bail/bond agreement. This made a Governor's Warrant possible. It was executed, and he was returned from Florida for incarceration.

In December, Mike and Danny located the third man named as a part of the group. Since this man was not the murderer, he also waived his rights and gave a sworn statement. He confirmed his presence at the sister's home when the four of them planned the robbery. He declared that it was Gary's sister who called for the Yellow Cab. Two male fares had guns. Gary used a revolver, and the young man (the first informer) carried both a sawed-off shotgun and a lug wrench. This witness claimed that his only part was operating the "trail car" (getaway vehicle).

He explained, "The cab arrived after midnight. Both, Gary and the informer, got into the back seat of the cab with their concealed weapons. As I walked to the getaway car, I saw the cabdriver's face and recognized him. [He had known the cabdriver for the past nine years, yet he did not intervene.] As I was following, the cab entered the cemetery. I knew there was a problem when the driver was forced out of his cab at gunpoint. Gary unbuckled the cabdriver's trousers so that he couldn't run from them as they searched him for a money belt. After finding no money, the informer struck the cabby in the head with his lug wrench." (Since information about a second head injury had not been made public, this verification substantiated the credibility of this witness.) Then both lifted the unconscious cabdriver and threw him upon the rear floor of the cab. Gary got into the driver's seat, and the young man went into the back with the victim. Gary drove the cab out of the cemetery and finally stopped in the South End of the city. I parked about halfway down the street, behind the cab. The cabdriver was now conscious, and they took him out of the cab, again at gunpoint. The cabdriver was standing with his pants around his ankles as Gary searched him once more. He was yelling, 'Where's the money.' The young man carrying the wrench was busy searching the inside of the cab when the cabby pulled a knife out of his jacket pocket and cut Gary's hand." (This explained the blood spots some distance from the body.)

The witness continued, "After that, he hitched up his pants and started running. The cabdriver did not make it very far before Gary caught him and threw him up against a fence. Gary pointed his gun to the back of the cabdriver's head and yelled, 'I should fuck you up for cutting me.' Then he fired his revolver!"

The witness also told the detectives that the shooter pulled the victim's pants down again while he was lying there helpless, bleeding from the head. This time, Gary allegedly made physical contact with both the victim's penis and rectal area. (Was this action to further denigrate the victim?) The executioner returned to the cab just as his accomplice was pulling a cigar box, full of money, from under the front passenger seat.

The getaway driver recalled driving both perpetrators to another location to split the money. He claimed his "take" was only some "reefers" and booze, but he did not protest his meager reward because Gary had already threatened him. He had been told, "If you tell anybody about this, I will personally kill you." The witness stated that he believed him.

From the statements made, the detectives established two photo arrays. Each set had to include photos that looked like the perpetrators. They found the necessary pictures in the record divisions at two different police stations. The "trail driver" identified all the parties involved. He also verified the crime scene photos.

The investigation continued. More incriminating facts added to the strength of their case. Witnesses confirmed a friendship between the accused parties. Some related direct conversations, which they had had with those accused. The victims of other robberies confirmed that similar types of weapons had been used against them, including the lug wrench. And of course, there was the fact that Gary and his sister had been arrested for a similar robbery. In all, the prosecuting attorney had a list of nineteen witnesses—a solid case!

All were convicted. The mother got her reward money, but she probably spent all of it on lawyers' fees for her son.

A diary note: *Cash... Those who have it or handle it are in constant jeopardy, but those who covet it are in greater danger for they lose their soul! The existence of such evil frightens me.*

Mike and Danny shared all their information with yet another police team who was working another unsolved robbery/murder. Their case involved an ATM bank card. The incident occurred at a bank machine near the courthouse on the very same day and around the same time that Gary and his sister had been released on bond—just before they disappeared. Needless to say, this case also culminated in guilty verdicts against Gary and his sister. The incredible thing about this case was that its conviction provided the mother with yet another $20,000 reward! It was because of her original input that this case was also solved.

My disbelief was boldly recorded: *She withheld the information until a reward was offered! She should have been arrested for obstruction of justice, not rewarded!* **Twice!**

CHAPTER 44

Medical Issues (1984–1985)

Once a detective, new injuries were few, but old injuries developed complications.

October 1984: Mike's left knee became so swollen that an ER doctor had to drain excess fluid. Medication was prescribed, and Mike was instructed to use icepacks. He walked out of the hospital on crutches.

November 1984: Mike again experienced shortness of breath and chest discomfort. An EKG verified a problem. The cause was his ileostomy! Blood test confirmed that excessive liquid fecal output had caused dehydration, which was responsible for a drop in his potassium level. This adversely affected his electrolyte balance. (Electrolytes regulate the heart.) Mike would have to begin a potassium regimen. A chest x-ray showed an elevated right diaphragm. It also affected his breathing capacity. This previously undetected paralysis was probably the result of a past cruiser accident. There was no treatment for it.

December 1984: Mike's partner was driving their unmarked unit when it was totaled. A woman did not yield to their siren and lights. She was attempting a left turn when she struck the detective vehicle head-on. Mike's right hand had contusions, and his left knee had a meniscus tear. His neck had a cervical strain and a compressed disc. Four months later, Mike's neck, right shoulder and right hand had not regained full strength. A specialist told Mike, "Expect a slow gradual resolution of the peripheral nerve contusion."

July 1985: Mike had another painful ileostomy blockage.

CHAPTER 45

Personal Memo (1985)

Mike was vice president of the Police Benevolent Association. The goal of the PBA was to assist officers, whether it be family medical bills or any other need. They also made donations to worthy causes, and once a year, they organized a huge picnic for officers' families. It was always a very successful affair.

Our children were now older and had made their own independent plans for the day, so I was looking forward to my date with Mike. As we were preparing to leave our house, the phone rang. I wanted to ignore it, but Mike went back to answer it. I was still sitting in the passenger seat when he gave me the bad news. "There has been a serious assault and the victim is being transported to the hospital."

I expressed my hope, "We can go to the picnic after you speak with him."

Mike slipped into the driver seat of his 1963 Corvette, and we were off—but our destination had changed.

Just twenty-five minutes later (a record trip), I found myself in the detective division. Mike had dropped me off and immediately left for the hospital. I first visited with the few remaining personnel, but everyone eventually left for the picnic, and I was left waiting alone for Mike's return. To pass the time, I read all the jokes posted on one bulletin board. On another, I read police directives and viewed mugshots. I circled the large division a dozen times before alighting at Mike's desk. Becoming bored, I searched a drawer for a piece of paper and a pen. What better way to relieve my frustration than to vent on paper? I wrote this poem:

> *To: Detective Mike,*
> *It is now 11:27 AM, Sunday, August 4, 1985.*
> *And at your neatly organized desk, here sit I,*
> *Gazing out of the window at a pretty blue sky,*
> *While you go off to the bedside of a man who may die.*
>
> *Earlier when the phone rang, I simply sighed.*
> *Knowing the police picnic would be put aside.*
> *But hoping our plans may somehow survive,*
> *I got into your Corvette to accompany you for the drive.*
>
> *I wanted to go to the crime scene and be at your side.*
> *Instead, you dropped me at the station to wait here inside!*
> *For the past sixteen years, I have had to abide,*
> *The waiting and wondering known to every police bride.*
>
> *Oh, the way you cops forget your own wives.*
> *It's a miracle any marriage ever survives!*
> *Upon this I pondered with misting blue eyes,*

Admitting we idiots adore you responsible guys.

Because of you, justice is often the victim's prize.
This is of greater importance, I theorize;
So for you, there will be no wifely demise.
Instead, I'll greet you with a smile in disguise!

1:45 PM: I'm trying to convince myself not to despise
The five-foot-eleven cop with the warm hazel eyes.
But the waiting and waiting starts my temper to rise.
Until..."Damn him! Damn this job!" are my ardent cries!
From: Abandoned Wife

After another half hour, Mike entered the empty detective division. He and his apology came through the door, "I'm sorry it took so long. I was hoping the victim would regain consciousness long enough to give me a statement."

"That's all right, I kept busy. I wrote a poem while I was waiting." I handed it up to him. Sitting on the edge of his desk, he read in silence. When he finished, understanding eyes met mine. His hand reached for mine as he declared, "Let's get the hell out of here!"

The victim had been admitted to the Intensive Care Unit. For now, we were on our way to enjoy the PBA picnic. The doctor would page Mike on his beeper if the victim regained consciousness!

Many dedicated officers become married to their job. Because they share the allure of excitement and the need for fraternity, the boys in blue become a substitute family. My diary warns: *A police wife must be ever diligent for the first signs of her husband's job consumption. He'll talk of little else but police business, and he will begin spending an hour (then two) drinking with the cloistered brotherhood after each shift. Against these symptoms she must act immediately. She must inspire the return of the man hidden behind the badge. I was too slow to act. I played the dedicated wife far too long! Now, like so many other cop's wives, I endure the loneliness by keeping very busy. In addition to managing our home with meals and laundry for four, I've used my seniority to acquire a six-and-a-half-hour school bus route. I'm also spending many hours negotiating a union contract. Occasionally, I write. While these pursuits are meant to be a buffer for the rejection I feel, I fear they are becoming a wedge enlarging the gap between us.*

CHAPTER 46

One of the Mass (1986)

In late August, a cruiser was dispatched to 97 Green Street at 8:30 AM. There had been a sudden death complaint. The first-floor resident met the officer and escorted him to the third-floor apartment, where a putrid decomposing male body was lying on a bed. The headboard and the wall were spattered with blood. The condition of the body made it impossible to predict the cause of death, so paramedics officially pronounced the occupant "dead at the scene" and removed the body to the morgue.

A patrolman was waiting for a locksmith when a man approached him and told him that he had loaned the deceased his car five days earlier, and the vehicle was missing. The officer made out a stolen car report while awaiting a new lock. Once installed, the officer took possession of the keys, thus securing the scene.

At 11:00 AM the next day, a state medical examiner performed an autopsy. His "post" labeled the death a homicide, as the result of multiple stab wounds (twenty). Mike and Pete were appointed as the lead investigating team. Several policemen met at the apartment. Measurements, photographs and articles were taken into evidence. Many people around the location were interviewed. When a friend of the victim arrived, he informed the officers that his brother, Harry, was using one of the bedrooms in the apartment. He pointed out his brother's room and his personal items. The last time he had seen either occupant was eight days earlier, when both men had dinner at his mother's house.

The detectives interviewed the mother, who confirmed that both her sons and the victim (a longtime friend) had come to her residence for supper at 5:00 PM. Harry and the victim had left at approximately 6:00 PM in a borrowed Cadillac. She said, "Harry's been staying with my friend since arriving from Boston, Massachusetts, three weeks ago. He told me he left Boston because of some trouble with a girl." Other witnesses declared they had not seen Harry since August 18, the day the borrowed vehicle had disappeared.

At 6:00 PM, Boston authorities were given a description of Harry as well as the stolen vehicle. They were also told that Harry had a girlfriend living in a nearby suburb and gave them her address. A half hour later, a Boston detective had information for them. His city had a valid sexual assault warrant for Harry, and the stolen vehicle was now parked outside the girlfriend's home. By 10:30 PM, Harry was in the custody of the Boston Police Department.

At 3:00 PM the next day, Mike and Pete were in Boston advising the suspect of his rights. (While taking his sworn statement, the detective noticed abrasions on Harry's hands. A witness would later explain.) Harry said he had returned to his hometown to seek employment. He was staying with a family friend, the victim. He stated, "After we got back from my mother's, this man made sexual passes at me, so I left the apartment and went to see a friend. When I got back around 11:30 PM, he called out to me from his bedroom. When I went into the bedroom to see what he wanted, he reached out for me and felt my body! It made me sick! I went into the kitchen and got a knife for protection. Then I went back into the bedroom to talk the problem out, but he came at me and grabbed my left arm. I stabbed him several times around the neck and face until he fell back onto the bed. I went into the bathroom. First, I washed my hands, but then decided to take a shower." When Harry returned into the bedroom, the victim was lying on the bed, blood-covered and motionless. Harry collected the knife, the car keys and a gold chain before departing. He said that he drove around for a while before deciding to seek sanctuary with an old girlfriend in Boston.

The old girlfriend's statement confirmed that Harry arrived at 6:00 AM. She said he was nervous and complained about his sore hands, which seemed to be cut. His right hand was very swollen. When she asked him what happened, Harry told her that there had been an altercation. Some guys had killed his uncle, so he used his uncle's car to get back to Boston.

The murder warrant was signed just three days after the body was found, and the investigation continued. The next week, Mike located the friend that Harry had visited on the night of the murder. This female witness relayed the fact that the suspect had been with her. "Harry left at 11:30 PM when my boyfriend got home, but he came back later around 3:30 AM all cleaned up." He had showered and changed his clothes.

Her boyfriend had much more to say! "When Harry returned, he told us he'd been locked out of his own apartment, so I told him he could sleep on the couch. Then I returned to the bedroom with my girlfriend and locked the door. A short time later, I heard Harry trying the knob. He called out, asking to speak with me. When I entered the living room, Harry grabbed me around the neck, but I managed to pull away. He then walked into the kitchen, saying he was just playing around, but when I joined him, he came at me with a knife. My hand was injured when I grabbed for the knife. [The plunging blade had broken off in his hand.] I called out to my girlfriend's brother, and he came to my rescue." Harry was ordered to leave, and he had not been seen since. The boyfriend had kept the broken knife and gave it to the detectives. He assured, "Harry had no reason to assault me. He was just acting weird."

Harry was incarcerated for twelve months before he was finally convicted. My diary notes: *US law declares justice must be swift, but the growing masses of criminals has jammed the judicial system. When criminals decry foul play on the civil rights field, it is only fitting that the penalty goes to their peers.*

Unfortunately, delayed trials impede justice. The longer a case takes to come to trial, the better the chance for acquittal. Witnesses move and their memories fade. Thus, the arresting officer's testimony becomes more important at a time when his vulnerability to err has increased. It is difficult to recall small details about a case which is a year old, and a good defense attorney will take this opportunity to bring about any minute slip in the hope that any discrepancy will damage the officer's credibility. More importantly, delays are unjust for the victims and their families. Without closure, their lives remain on hold in hell.

CHAPTER 47

Reinjured

February 1986: Mike and his partner were absorbed in a conversation as they walked down a police station corridor. They were on their way to their desks to write up reports about the progress made in their current murder case. It would be the first time that the state would allow a suspect to be charged for murder without a body. (The husband had used a wood-chipper machine.) When they approached the detective division, the door hurled open and slammed into Mike's face. This time the worker's compensation insurance would be paying for a three-cap bridge. After that incident, the door was replaced by one which had a window.

October 1986: Mike reinjured his left knee while wrestling a suspect to the ground to make an arrest. The ER diagnosis: Internal derangement of the left knee. Orthoscopic surgery was required. After the reconstruction of the ligament was achieved, the knee was declared to have 15 percent permanent partial disability.

Mike's shoulder was reevaluated. The nerve damage had not improved. There was some paralysis over the right pectoralis. Mike's right upper extremity was declared a 10 percent permanent partial disability.

How much bad luck could one man have?

CHAPTER 48

Certified Mistress (1987)

The mailman delivered a notice of death—the death of a commitment. It was an ordinary envelope. My name and address were handwritten. Since there was no return address, I assumed it to be correspondence from either a friend or family member. Opening it with joyful anticipation only added to my shock as my wide eyes delivered the shot that pierced my heart.

Toni immediately proclaimed that she was Mike's mistress. To prove this to be a fact, she expounded intimate details. She knew of Mike's abdominal surgery, which left him with a permanent ileostomy (a condition normally kept secret). Toni's knowledge of our family's personal problems mirrored Mike's interpretation. Her open privilege to these matters hurt me deeply, for I had (until now) presumed these things to be privately shared only between Mike and myself. I felt totally betrayed!

My diary relays: *Toni took great pleasure in telling me that, unlike me, she fulfills all of his sexual needs and has been doing so for some time!* It was that spiteful statement that gave me insight into the complete picture. Apparently, Mike was not ready to cut the marital strings, and she had become impatient. Clearly, she intended to force the issue. Well, she succeeded!

Her letter of doom was still in my hand when I heard my rivaling offspring entering from the back of the house. Thank God. Their voices acted like surgical heart paddles forcing my heart to return to normal rhythm and my mind out of shock. I was able to conceal Toni's weapon in my pocket just in time to greet my children. Fortunately, they both planned to leave soon. (Good!) They would be gone before their father arrived.

My temper was under control by the time Mike got home (late again). As he sat removing his shoes in the kitchen, I calmly stated, "I got a surprising letter today."

His response was normal. "Oh, from who?" The second shoe hit the floor.

With a false calm, I handed it to him. "Here, you can read it yourself."

In seconds, his face grew taut. His eyes sped across the paper. **Silence, guilty silence** permeated the room.

Time had allowed me to consider my options, so it was with calm dignity that I pronounced his sentence, "I want you out of the house by the first of the month. I only have one question. Was Toni always a shrew, or has she become one because of you?" (The question was rhetorical.) I quietly walked out of the room. To be able to pull off such a seemingly unruffled exit restored a bit of my pride.

The next day, I composed my own letter:

> *Dear Toni,*
>
> *I wish to express my sorrow for your pain, for someone who writes such a hateful letter must surely be suffering. With such pain, I can understand your instinct to strike out, but I*

regret that you have chosen me as your target. You and Mike are to blame, not I. Both of you are committing adultery. Therefore, you must both accept responsibility for your own pain. I hope your hate will not cloud this truth from you.

*With regret for **all** of our pain, I remain,*

June

P.S. I am entrusting Mike to deliver this letter to you as I do not know your address. I have told him that he owes me that much.

My diary describes my misery during the following months:

I have been fighting many psychological battles.
1. *Self-incrimination vs. self-righteousness.*
2. *Loneliness vs. privacy.*
3. *Self-pity vs. determination.*
4. *Worthlessness vs self-worth.*

*I have come through this personal hell the victor, for I find myself in possession of my sanity, my pride and my compassion, and I have gained a new quality—resiliency. The death knell is for a twenty-five-year-old marriage commitment. But the death of one commitment has given birth to a new commitment, **me.***

A feeling of self-worth gave me the courage to live alone. I did it, just like hundreds of other police wives whose husbands had succumbed. Why had infidelity become such a phenomenal demon within the police community? The endless opportunities. Many females find the macho mystique of a police-man alluring. Grateful women, helped by officers, find it easy to develop a friendship with their knights in shining armor. Adventurous groupies freely flirt and even offer sexual favors. In addition, irregular work schedules lend feasible alibis to those officers wishing to explore!

CHAPTER 49

A New Beginning (1988)

Sunday morning, I awoke to the sound of movement in the house. Since the dog had not barked, I knew it had to be my estranged husband. Even though he had left me for a much-younger woman, he had reserved Sundays for me. Every week he showed up to repair anything necessary around the house, which was now deeded solely in my name. He gave me money for bills that exceeded my paychecks. He cleaned my car inside and out, and often took me out for dinner, over which I would update him about our son and daughter. (Lonny was in college, and Lori was living with a boyfriend.) I enjoyed these days and often thought that Mike was treating me more decently now than he had when we were still living together.

When Mike first left me, I had told him that I would not divorce him. My diary notes: *I told him that I needed his health insurance plan and wanted to claim any financial rights which were privileged to a wife should he be killed on the job. I feel that I deserve that financial security. It is my rightful reward for my twenty-five years of nursing care and complete fidelity. Only once did I discover an enticing attraction, but I never allowed myself to act upon that forbidden impulse. I also told him that a divorce would be forthcoming only if I found someone else to love, and if I decided to remarry.*

In a mutual separation agreement, I have agreed not to claim any of his accumulated retirement funds. This was in exchange for him removing his name from our home's deed. Other than that, I only asked him for $50 a week. (Mike gives me more.) Together we went to one attorney who drew up a legal contract.

Within the last year, Mike has not once sought to change that arrangement, but he and his mistress have purchased a three-story tenement house in the city.

I glanced at my bedside clock and was surprised to find that it was only 6:00 AM. He was certainly getting an early start! The aroma of coffee influenced me to leave my comfortable bed. When I entered the kitchen, he was nowhere in sight, so I presumed he had already started some project in the garage. My presumption was wrong. Mike reentered the house carrying a large bundle over his shoulder. He passed me without a word and entered the living room. I followed with a cup of coffee in hand. There, he laid down a huge pile of hangers draped with clothing. Incredulous! Was this his way of saying that he wanted to move back in? My first utterance was a vindictive retort, "So it wasn't greener on the other side of the pasture?"

Unprovoked, Mike's eyes met mine as he simply asked, "Do you want me to leave?"

I stood there in dishabille—my T-shirt in wrinkles, my hair in disarray. But my physical appearance was less of a mess than my tumultuous brain. I had to look away from Mike's eyes so that I could think. He merely remained silent as I studied my bare feet. When my eyes finally regained his, my heart forced out a whisper, "No."

And so it was that Mike and I started a new beginning. I confided my fear to my diary: *Time will tell if we succeed. A sacred trust once broken is difficult to mend.*

CHAPTER 50

Unsolicited Advice (1988)

Mike and I were happy that our son, now twenty-three, had successfully graduated from college with a 3.74 GPA in business administration. I enjoyed a sense of relief and set aside my fears that Lonny would jump into his father's police boots. For me, coping with one cop in the family was hard enough.

Lonny had found local employment as an accountant. He was proud of landing a job with a prestigious certified public accounting firm, one of the "Big Eight". Lisa, now his wife, had graduated from college and was starting her career in special education. Everything was perfect. (I should have known that it was just *too* good to be true!) Before long, Lonny became bored with accounting. He could not stand being restricted to a desk all day. Like his father, he decided to forsake his first career and applied to the police academy! Knowing the resistance to my son's decision would be futile, I voiced only two thoughts. The first confirmed my disappointment. "Lonny, we sent you to college so that you wouldn't follow in your father's footsteps." My other statement revealed my quiet resignation, "Lisa must really love you. She thought she was marrying a CPA not a COP."

After only a few days in training, Lonny came home highly agitated. I immediately inquired, "What's wrong?"

Lonny was appalled by classmates who openly displayed their prejudice toward minorities. He seethed with righteous indignation. To explain, he repeated some of their disgusting comments, then relayed what had been his spontaneous rejoinder, **"Stupid rednecks!"** Hearing this caused me instant concern. Making enemies of fellow cadets was not only unwise but dangerous. One day, Lonny may need to depend upon them for backup; instead, he may get payback. On the street, a fellow officer could take an extra few minutes responding to a scene. He could make sure he was not the first one through a door. He could lag behind during a joint foot chase. Many spiteful acts could be accomplished without ever raising any suspicions about their malicious intent.

Lonny's story kept darting through my mind. I worried that he did not grasp the significance of the incident. Even though he was an adult, I felt it was my duty as a caring mother to warn him about the danger of alienation. Because my success was paramount, I carefully deliberated the best approach. I decided upon this note:

> *Lonny,*
>
> *It is now 12:32 AM, and I lie in bed making mental notes of the things I must do tomorrow (today). I have placed priority upon a conversation with you, but second thoughts have persuaded me to write you this note instead. You see, I'm not sure that you will be receptive to my suggestion. By putting it into writing, you cannot interrupt with immediate rejection but will be forced into more careful consideration.*

You take after your parents in that you are self-confident. This is good but you must beware (as must I) not to allow self-confidence to turn into self-righteousness. A self-righteous person only has the ability to **react**. *A self-confident person has the ability to* **respond**.

Reacting vs. Responding: The first is spontaneous, immediate and without thought. The latter allows constraint, consideration and contemplation. If you do not merely react but learn to respond, you will succeed in both mental and physical control. This control is your protection.

Those prejudice cadets of whom you spoke, may one day (night) be the people upon whom your life depends. It is unwise to alienate them. Instead of reacting to their prejudices, it would be better to respond to them? With contemplated response you have a chance to sway their opinions. Since a picture is worth a thousand words, create that picture. Demonstrate your acceptance of any man because of his merit. Thoughtless reaction seldom brings any profitable results. Name calling is useless. The streets are dangerous. You had best not make more enemies than those who are already out there.

Please respond (not react) to this, your mother's self-confident (not self-righteous) opinion. Your contemplation will be my fruitful reward and your profitable gain.

I love you,
Mom

Because all mothers want their children to be safe, they experience an intuitive fear. If your child is a policeman, that fear is intensified. As a maternal scribe, I noted: *I find some relief knowing Lonny stays physically fit. He works out; jogs and plays softball, soccer and hockey.* (A few years later, he earned a purple karate belt for self-defense.)

CHAPTER 51

Uncooperative Murder Suspect (1988)

In early December 1988, Mike initiated the arrest of a murder suspect. A fight ensued. During the fracas, Mike was kicked and beaten, but eventually got the assailant into a headlock. They were in that position as both went tumbling down a flight of stairs. Mike's stubbornness gave him the strength to maintain the headlock until help placed the man in handcuffs. Mike told arriving EMTs, "I'm getting too old for this shit."

At the emergency room, doctors once again listed reinjuries to his left knee, back and neck. A new body part was added to the list. The left distal bicep was ruptured. The doctor told Mike that surgery would not be successful. (Such surgery had not been perfected back then.) Mike returned to work January 24, 1989.

A diary note: *These injuries will allow Mike to be home for Christmas this year.*

CHAPTER 52

Cold Case Conspiracy (1989)

This old unsolved homicide actually occurred while Mike was still a patrolman in uniform. It had happened in the summer of 1980. Mike procured the nine-year-old file: At 1:00 AM, the police department had been notified about a shooting. ER doctors treated a female victim named Irene, who had been transported to their nearby hospital in her brother's car. She suffered gunshot wounds to her head and one hand. The hospital reported information about another male victim who was still at 216 Bradley Street. One cruiser was dispatched to the hospital, while another was sent to the reported address.

When the officer entered the home, the second victim was found lying face down on the floor in the living room. The victim's face was in a pool of blood. He had no vital signs. His body showed no signs of postmortem lividity (blood settling in the body). This victim had just recently died. Just before 2:00 AM, an investigating team arrived with one forensic detective. The victim was identified as Wyatt. He was heavy-set, dressed in black slacks and a light shirt. Nearby were two pairs of pants and two suit jackets with their pockets turned inside out. Still upon the body were two gold chains, a gold wristwatch and rings. More jewelry and coins were on the coffee table. Also in view, within the living room, were spent shells (.45 caliber). A blood trail led from the living room to the kitchen, then into the bathroom. Evidence was secured while photos and measurements were taken.

Outside, the victim's Cadillac remained parked in the driveway. From their observations, the investigators believed that this was no simple robbery/murder.

1. The perpetrators had been looking for something specific. (Had they found it?)
2. The assailants probably thought they had killed both parties.

The brother of the female victim left the hospital and returned to the address of the crime scene to assist the police. He told an officer that he and others had been waiting for his sister, Irene, outside in his car when they heard the gunshots. Three white males immediately exited the house and left the neighborhood in a white Buick. He described its unusual markings.

The initial investigation was completed, so the detectives locked the doors with the victim's set of keys and left. This proved to be the first mistake made in this case. Years later, Mike would wonder if the investigators had requested a uniformed patrolman be posted there. The Field Service Division could have denied their request because of money or manpower shortages. A patrolman's presence would not only have protected the crime scene but would also have saved investigators unnecessary paperwork. Now, if detectives needed to return into the home seeking more evidence, they would first have to obtain a warrant. (Once a crime scene is vacated, a warrant must be approved allowing re-entry.)

Back at the hospital, officers learned about Irene's miraculous luck. She had not been killed because one of the lethal bullets had lodged itself in her left hand, which had been positioned over her head. The other projectile had penetrated through the same hand but had ricocheted in such a way that it only grazed the lower back of her skull. It only knocked her unconscious. That was a blessing, for no more bullets were fired into her body. Fearing that the assassins would learn she was still alive, Irene signed herself out of the hospital at 4:00 AM, just a few hours after being shot. (She had an appointment to have the embedded bullet removed from her hand later that day.)

At 5:55 PM, Irene was transported from the hospital by cruiser number 26. At the police department, she described the entire incident. Her brother had driven her to Wyatt's home because she wanted to stop by and repay him one hundred dollars, which she had borrowed. As she stepped through the door, someone instantly grabbed her and threw her to the floor. The male victim called out to her, "Scream!" (to make noise), but one of the suspects shoved something into her mouth. Although she had been told to keep her face down, she spied two white male suspects. She also heard a third man's voice. The younger man, in view, was six feet tall and wore a plaid shirt and blue jeans. The older one was shorter, five foot seven. He had a mustache and wore glasses. These two men continued beating Wyatt and asking, "Where's the five thousand dollars? Where's the coke?"

The other assailant said, "Let's kill them both. Let's stick pins in their ears." Then she heard a shot, and the beaten victim lay on the floor next to her not moving. A few seconds later, she felt a blow to the back of her head. It rendered her unconscious. When she regained consciousness, the perpetrators were gone. She first staggered into the kitchen, then wandered out toward her brother's car.

At daylight, the detectives went back to Wyatt's to better canvass the crime scene. When they arrived, a police cruiser and several people were present. Neighbors had reported a B&E (break and enter). Wyatt had only been dead for a few hours, but the vultures had already gained access into his home through a cellar window. Everyone was identified. All were family members! They were taking his possessions: a television, a record player, furniture and personal items. Since the detectives had not returned with a warrant (their second mistake), they could not prevent the man's "loving" family from taking away what they had already loaded into their cars and one truck. But the officers did prevent further pilfering by once again sealing off the home, this time for the purpose of probate. When the victim's daughter asked for her father's car keys, she was informed that she would have to go through probate court to get them. Now that the crime scene had been breached, even the items still left inside would be useless as evidence. All would be considered tainted!

Over the years, several investigators followed different trails, but none led to the end of this homicide investigation. In fact, it seemed that each newly explored avenue only made the maze more complicated. No routes linked to lead them in the right direction. By the time Mike took an interest, there were many challenging dead ends. He wanted to be the one to break down the barriers and make the connections. He wanted to be the one to solve this dual murder/attempted murder case.

Upon review, Mike was immediately aware of three aspects:

1. The case was a "cluster fuck" (Mike's personal term used to describe the many mistakes made).
2. He knew some of the "players" (people involved).
3. Hundreds of pieces of information had to be organized.

Mike began by dividing all the previous information into categories: evidence, witnesses, victim's associates, police background reports, etc. Once organized, he had a clear view of the puzzle's pieces. Mike and his partner set out to confirm those pieces already in hand. They contacted every investigator who had ever worked on the case, even those who had since retired. From interviews with these detectives, Mike not only confirmed data he had found in the file, but he discovered that some information, once in the file, was now missing. Certain written reports had disappeared. Mike also gleaned new knowledge. He was verbally entrusted with information which had never been written into the police file because, at the time, these tidbits had seemed unrelated to the case.

Mike and his partner then checked to make sure that none of the initial forensic evidence was missing. After finding it still intact, they proceeded to the category of known associates. They reviewed each witnesses' statement, along with its attached police background statement. From Wyatt's associates, it was determined that the man had been a self-employed "booster" (a fence, a middleman). His expertise at finding both goods and buyers was well-known in local circles. Buyers were not leery of purchasing stolen goods from him. At times, potential buyers even asked him to find specific items for them. To sell his goods, he hung out in specific places to make sales contacts. He favored a couple of bars and one popular restaurant. It was strange that he chose that particular restaurant because it was also a favorite place for district patrolmen to eat. (This restaurant did not charge policemen for their food.) Mike had often eaten there when he was a patrolman, but he would always pay a portion of his nonexisting tab, and he always tipped the waitresses. Mike discovered that one of those waitresses had been

Irene, the surviving victim, and another waitress had been her sister.

Searching for associates and friends of both victims brought Mike and his partner to that location. They were lucky. They found Irene's sister still employed as a waitress. She was willing to talk to Mike because she remembered him well. (She had always appreciated his tips.) Mike's past acquaintance was advantageous. He was able to persuade her of his interest in bringing these criminals to justice. He told her, "To do that I need to find Irene. Without her, it's useless." The waitress explained her reluctance to help. She believed the 1980 investigation had been mishandled, perhaps on purpose. She said that the initial detectives broke appointments with her sister. When they did show up, they brought photos of people with absolutely no resemblance to the description Irene had given them. It was not long before mistrust of the police caused her to flee the state. Irene had been on the move ever since.

Mike assured the waitress that he would never place her sister in jeopardy and asked if she would speak to Irene on his behalf. He even suggested a safe method of contact. Irene could leave him voice mail using a fictitious name. Mike promised to meet Irene at any time and at any place of her choosing. The waitress stipulated that Mike's partner could not know the false name being used, nor could anyone else come with him to the meet. Since Mike agreed, she acquiesced, and they privately agreed upon the name "Mary Beth". Mike left the restaurant with a positive feeling. Irene would contact him, but he had to be careful. He only had circumstantial evidence leading to the assailants' identities. This surviving witness was the key for prosecution. He did not want her to disappear again. When Irene did not make contact, he did not push her.

In the meantime, he and his partner had a lot more work to do. Mike wanted all the information he could get before talking with this frightened victim. She would have no confidence if he were not knowledgeable. If he demonstrated that he knew what he was doing, maybe then she would trust him. Irene did call! But she was still afraid to arrange a meeting. During the next month, she and Mike talked a few times on the phone. Mike shared whatever facts he could with her, so she began to share her information with him. She described the car parked in front of Wyatt's house the night of the shooting, and she precisely described two of the three assailants. She stated, "I'll never forget their faces." From her input and that of Wyatt's past associates, Mike hoped to be able to establish photo arrays of possible suspects.

Sometime after Wyatt's death, the FBI had discovered a secret business associate in New York City. Their investigation disclosed Wyatt's involvement in an interesting business deal. It seemed Wyatt received stolen black gold from aircraft employees. (Their factory used the substance to line engines.) After paying these parties for the substance, Wyatt had sent it to a metal company, which was paid to melt out its impurities. The gold was then sold to a New York jeweler.

In this city, Wyatt had known associates who were "ladies of the night". To seek out information about these prostitutes, Mike went to a friend who was assigned to vice and narcotics. Mike was surprised to find out that his friend had personal knowledge about the case. Detective James assured Mike that he had submitted a written report to "homicide" just weeks after the murder. Fortunately, James was able to find his copy of that report. Strange…Mike had found no such report in the case file! It relayed information the detective had received from a prostitute. She had stolen five thousand dollars and some cocaine from members of an organized criminal group; then used the money to pay Wyatt. She had also given him the drugs to sell—agreeing to an equal split. Shortly before Wyatt died, owners of the stolen property had found her. The family threatened to kill her if she did not tell them where their property was. Needless to say, she fingered the booster. Wyatt had promised that he would return their losses, but he needed time to raise the money. Bingo! One could assume his time had run out. This information not only confirmed the motive for the execution, but also named the people responsible for the act.

Mike and his partner now sought to locate this prostitute so that they could corroborate their new information—information which should have already been a documented fact. Police computers located her. She was currently incarcerated in another state. Arrangements were made for an interview, and Mike and his partner traveled to the prison. She verified everything learned from Detective James. While Mike was happy to confirm her information, he was unhappy about the missing police report. Why was this piece of the puzzle missing? Had it simply been misplaced between divisions, or had it been purposely diverted into the hands of the involved mafia family? Who would have done such a thing?

Other prostitutes had knowledge of this criminal family as well. When located, they stated that they knew about the criminals being ripped off. They also relayed information about an out-of-state yacht party that had taken place around the same time. In attendance was a certain city police detective. (Pictures might be available.) To Mike's knowledge, this information had never been entered into previous police files either. Did the named detective have an illegal association with this criminal group? Did he smother the case on their behalf? Even if pictures could be located, did they prove anything? Mike, himself, often had occasion to have conversation with bad guys. Had IAD (Internal Affairs Division) been aware of a clandestine association? Had the detective been working undercover?

A new piece to the puzzle arrived unexpectedly. Mike received a collect call from Mr. Simmons. Although the name was unfamiliar, Mike accepted the call. (Incarcerated criminals could only make telephone calls by calling collect.) If this was a call from some jail or prison, it probably meant someone wanted to trade information for sentence time. In the past, this type of "pipeline" had proven very helpful. Even though Mr. Simmons was imprisoned, he was aware that Mike was working on Wyatt's old murder case. (The criminal grapevine is incredible!) He said he had some interesting information, which he would share if it would reduce his burglary sentence. As always, Mike made no promises but did tell Mr. Simmons that if his information lead to a conviction, he would see what he could do for him. Mr. Simmons took Mike at his word and agreed to be interviewed. Since Mike was now aware that this case could be leading into murky water, he used extreme caution when arranging their meeting. He called a correctional supervisor whom he knew and trusted. Mike explained that he did not want to question Mr. Simmons in one of the usual conference stalls, because the entire prison population would learn about it. The supervisor agreed to remove the caller under the false pretense that he had to appear in court for a hearing. Trusted guards would remove him to an isolated area at that same prison.

During the interview, Mr. Simmons gave a signed sworn statement verifying that he had worked for the mafia. He knew two brothers and a nephew. Mr. Simmons admitted his involvement in their very lucrative burglary ring. One brother would set up specific targets while he, the nephew and one other party (currently incarcerated) committed the burglaries. After several burglaries, he learned how one brother chose the locations. Allegedly, information was received via a lawyer/politician. A lot of this attorney's business involved housecalls to the well-to-do elderly, so he was very familiar with his clients' homes. He was aware of their layouts, cognizant of their security systems and apprised of their valuable possessions. (Was this lawyer/politician actively involved?) The man's son was known as troublesome. Could he have breached his father's files? At that point, Mr. Simmons paused and suggested, "Now, let's see what you can do for me."

Mike replied, "The politician died last year. The statute of limitations has run out on some of the burglaries you have mentioned, and you aren't in jail because of any of the others mentioned. I need more before approaching the State Attorney about any deal."

Several minutes passed in silence while their mind game continued. Finally, Mr. Simmons said, "I have more." He went on to state that he had been in the presence of both family bothers and the nephew when they were discussing how they had killed Wyatt and his girlfriend. (They had assumed Irene was his girlfriend.) Simmons stated that he had been given the task of destroying the family's Buick, which had been at the crime scene. He described special things about the car, which confirmed the description already given by Irene, her brother and Wyatt's neighbors. He explained that he drove the car to a certain location, made it appear as if it had been stolen, and then burned it. After he reported his job done, the family then reported it stolen. Since the vehicle had been so badly burned, it had no value. Therefore, it was towed to a local junkyard and crushed.

Mike went to the town that Mr. Simmons had named. There, the police department confirmed his story with records of a burned Buick. It had been recovered on the same date that Mr. Simmons had specified, and it had been owned by the family he had named. It was the same make and model as the car involved in the murder. Since the family lived in that town, Mike asked the local police to check their arrest records also. Luck was riding on Mike's shoulder. From those files, he was able to procure pictures of all three family members, and the photos dated back to the same time period as the murder! With them, Mike made two photo arrays: one for the older brothers, and one for the younger nephew. (Photo arrays must be constructed with pictures of individuals sharing similar appearances, nationality, sex, age, etc.) Mr. Simmons identified all three parties.

Mike and his partner took the same two photo arrays out of state. They traveled back to the imprisoned prostitute who had once stolen from this family. She identified the men also. They were the same people that Simmons had worked with. Hoping to make a deal herself, she also offered more information. She said that the family was in the same type of "booster" business as Wyatt. They were not only upset with Wyatt because of the stolen five thousand dollars and drugs, but also because they wanted in on some big gold scam he had been working.

In the midst of all this, the hiding victim held two secret meetings with Mike, but now he had to convince her to allow his partner to be present. Mike first assured Irene that he would bring a female detective whom they could trust. He then explained why he wanted her at the interview: He had two photo arrays to show Irene. If she was able to pick out her assailants, he wanted another police officer present as a witness. His partner would then be able to verify that proper procedure had been followed and could later testify (if necessary) about how identifications were made. Irene agreed to meet them.

Remembering Mike's previous advice, she selected a busy public place in which to meet.

Mike was becoming uneasy about possible subterfuge. Throughout the investigation, many of his associates had advised him to drop his inquisition. Initially, he presumed the advice was well intended. Those who had bothered to expound said things like "Most of the players are shitheads, so why bother yourself?" or "Mike, you're getting into dangerous territory." Even that certain partying detective had told him, "Forget it." At the time, Mike thought his comment was made only because he had not succeeded in solving the case himself. Now he wondered if there was another reason. Was it meant to be earnest advice or a subtle warning? Paranoid or not, it was better to be safe than sorry! Mike felt obligated to protect this victim from any further harm. He personally took care of the traveling arrangements and did not disclose the name of the state, the town, or the bar chosen for the meet.

It turned out that Irene really had not forgotten the two assailants' faces, last seen nine years before. From one photo array, she immediately picked out the nephew as the shooter. From the second, she identified the uncle. **This case was solved!** Mike took pride in his accomplishment, and his partner, a relatively new detective, was happy about everything she had learned along the way.

Their joy was short-lived. The state's chief prosecuting attorney refused Mike's request for an arrest warrant! Mike was shocked. He had been granted hundreds of warrants during his career. He had an excellent reputation for presenting only credible cases, and his requests were usually granted quickly. Normally, a mere ten-minute review of facts was all that was required. Only once before had he been denied. (That case also implicated a politician.) He thought, *They don't want to open any avenues which might lead to corruption.* But out loud he uttered an incredulous, **"Why?"** The excuses for denial were an insult to his intelligence, and he rebuked every reason declared to him. When Mr. Simmons's credibility was questioned, Mike explained that he had already confirmed every point that the convict had made. Mike suggested the chief prosecutor could personally corroborate one of the burglaries. All he had to do was call his own father, a judge, whose home had been burglarized by this same group. Instead, the man gave one final excuse, "We need the victim, and she'll never come in to testify." His answer remained steadfast, "No!" Since this prosecutor's own father had lost an expensive piece of art to these criminals, he should have been especially interested in nailing this family for murder. Why not?

Mike had no choice. He had to accept the fact that there would be no prosecution. **He would not look upon it as <u>his</u> failure. He had solved this case!** Mike was insulted, disappointed and furious. It took a couple of beers to subdue his anger. Once returned to a calmer state, he reviewed the debacle in his mind. With reflection, he began to think maybe it was for the best. Irene was still alive and probably had a better chance of staying that way if she did not come in for a trial. He hoped his investigation gave her an even better chance, because now, she knew who she was running from. Was he rationalizing? Without prosecution, these criminals would be free to continue pursuing her. Would they do so with renewed vigor because of his investigation? Had he abetted these criminals and put Irene in further jeopardy? Was **that** the ugly truth? God, he hoped not. I knew what Mike was feeling. *"I'm sorry, Irene. I failed you."*

After a couple more beers, Mike's emotional turmoil was quelled by an innovative decision. From now on, he would be smart and just float along. After all, it was both physically and emotionally healthier if one did not become so involved. In just one more year, he would have his twenty years, the minimum requirement for retirement. He declared, "Floaters nev'r get hurt, and they nev'r get in trouble with the brass. I'm gon'a just float right along int'a ratirement."

A few days later, Mike's inebriated resolution eluded him when a new homicide case came in. His innate morals would not allow him to become a "floater".

Diary thoughts: *The police profession offers tantalizing thrills! Just like a roller coaster, it provides extreme highs and speedy lows. Both are detrimental to one's equilibrium. I fear the family's emotions are too easily car-jacked and taken along for the ride.*

Note: To my knowledge, this case is still designated **unsolved**.

CHAPTER 53

Curveballs (1989)

By the end of 1989, Lori had given us two beautiful grand-children, both quite burdensome due to medical problems. My granddaughter had been born in 1987 with ear infections. When she was only three weeks old, she was back in the hospital screaming with pain from a spinal tap, which was needed to confirm whether or not the ear infection had spread into her brain. It had not. For several days, Lori lived at the hospital, nursing Sherrelle every three hours. Finally, the massive doses of IV antibiotics got the situation under control; but through-out Sherrelle's first year, ear infections constantly reoccurred. It seemed antibiotics were a normal part of her diet until her ear canals grew large enough for ear tubes. At eleven months, she was big enough for an ear specialist to implant her first set of tubes. A second set was put in a year later. Another problem existed as well. There were periods of screaming followed by projectile vomiting. Since Lori had stopped breastfeeding, the pediatrician suggested sensitivity to her formula and ordered a soy formula. But the problem continued every now and then. At the age of ten, a neurologist would diagnose migraine headaches. He also suggested that her earlier projectile vomiting had probably been due to migraines.

Her brother was born in 1989. Unfortunately, Lori decided not to nurse my grandson and soon found out that he was allergic to both milk and soy formulas. His reaction to them was so severe that he suffered with bleeding intestines (colitis). When only one month old, a gastroenterologist prescribed medication and a special whey formula. This corrected that problem, but Spencer would also need ear tubes and medication for asthma and allergies.

Lonny and Lisa had been married in 1987 and lived with us until they had saved for the down payment for their own home. In December 1989, Lonny's entire class (forty-two police officers) had been laid off due to the city's financial crisis. Lonny and a few other officers found work in a nearby city. (He is now a captain.) At the same time, Lisa changed jobs. She took a position at a public junior high school. From the children's facility where she had previously worked, she took one five-year-old Puerto Rican foster child named Roberto. Her teaching and caring had brought this abused child out of his shell, and he had begun to speak! Mike and I enjoyed this third grandchild as well. All was going well until Lisa and Lonny had their own child. When their daughter, Danielle, was born in 1990, Roberto was extremely jealous. After he displayed hostility toward the newborn, Lisa and Lonny were forced to cancel their adoption plans and made arrangements for him to leave. Lisa cried as they drove away from his new foster home. Two years later, they would have their own son. At Chad's birth, he was immediately diagnosed with pneumonia. His first week was spent in the pediatric intensive care unit because he had swallowed fluid during his birth.

Diary note: *Life is full of curveballs, so it takes a patient player to await the right pitch. Even then, a home run rarely comes to fruition, so we must be content with our base hits. The trick is to find joy in playing the game—living our lives.*

CHAPTER 54

Regrets (1990)

The telephone rang just as I was inserting my key into the door-knob. I picked it up on the third ring. "May I speak to Mike?" asked the young man. I told the caller that Mike was not there and asked if I could take a message. When Pedro identified himself, my face smiled in recognition. "Pedro! I'm so sorry. I didn't recognize your voice." (It had been well over a year and a half since I had last spoken to him.) The boy was calling to give Mike his latest telephone number.

Mike had met Pedro when the youngster was barely one year old. His older brother, Daniel, was just three. They had met under unpleasant circumstances. When Mike was still a patrolman, he had been dispatched to a tenement in his North End district to investigate a domestic complaint. He found a battered young woman. Her boyfriend "put her in her place". Mike's heart went out to her two small boys. They were ter-rorized, so Mike assured them that everything was going to be all right. They, of course, did not believe him because they had witnessed other battering incidents. Daniel cried, "He'll come back!" Pedro just cried. Their anguish compelled Mike to promise that he would make sure the brute never returned. He informed the boys that he patrolled their district all the time, and that he would be stopping in to check on them. With that promise, Mike wiped the tears from their cheeks.

While transporting the assailant to the police department, Mike made it perfectly clear what he thought of a man who would beat a woman. He also told the perpetrator that he would be taking a personal interest in this battered family, and that it would be in the man's own best interest to leave them alone. Mike warned, "I'm going to check on them every day." Mike kept his promise. Once the children began to feel safe, his visits became less frequent, once a week.

Two years later, Mike asked me if he could bring both boys home for a weekend visit. Since Lonny (then age thirteen) and Lori (then age eleven) would be expected to help entertain the young ones, their opinion was sought as well. It was agreed. Mike would pick them up on a Saturday morning and return them Sunday afternoon.

About eleven o'clock, I heard Mike's car pulling into the driveway. I went to the back door to meet the dirtiest three- and five-year-old I had ever seen! Before I had a chance to say anything, Mike informed me that he had already told the boys that the first event of the day would be a nice warm bath. While Mike stripped off their crusty clothes, Lonny started the bath water, and Lori located the newly purchased bath toys. I started lunch so that Pedro and Daniel could eat just as soon as they were clean. I did not have to hurry. The boys were having so much fun playing that Mike added hot water to their bath twice before their stomachs finally persuaded them to get out.

Their mother had provided a second set of clothes, but I had also thrown those into the washer. Since everything was still tumbling in the dryer, each dressed for lunch in one of Mike's big T-shirts. Both boys devoured their sandwiches and asked for more junk food—potato chips. Afterward, Lonny played "Go Fish" with Daniel while Lori found paper and crayons to entertain little Pedro. As our guests glowed in the limelight, Mike and I glowed with pride because of the wonderful way our children were responding to these less-fortunate little boys. Later, everyone went to the park. On the way home, Mike suggested supper at a pizzeria, and all heartily expressed their approval.

By the time we got home, everyone was exhausted from the busy day. I oversaw the washing of little hands and faces. As I went searching for extra toothbrushes, Mike helped the boys into the same big T-shirts, which would be used in lieu of pajamas. Teeth were brushed before they hopped onto the couch to cuddle. Before I finished reading *Pinocchio*, Pedro had fallen fast asleep. Daniel wanted to hear a second book!

The next morning, they were up at dawn—just like most small children. I fed them pancakes, bacon and orange juice. As soon as they had finished, they requested another bath! They wanted to play with their new toys again. After these little prunes were removed from the tub, they dressed and went into the fenced-in backyard to play ball with the dog. Daniel took interest in the fragrant lilac bushes and asked if he could bring some home to his mom. Mike boosted him up onto his shoulders, and together they gathered a large bouquet. The weekend had been a great success. Another sleepover was repeated on Thanksgiving. The following year, they spent Christmas Day. One summer, the boys spent three days with our family at the beach. It was heartwarming to watch them running away from the waves and constructing their first sandcastle. Over the years, Mike kept in touch. He would check how school was going and delivered birthday presents. Sometimes he would lose contact because they periodically moved, but sooner or later,

Mike would run into a family member who would give him an update.

When Pedro was twelve and Daniel was fourteen, they were taken away from their mother and placed in the state's care. They now had a young sister, but she was placed with relatives. At that time, Pedro had left a number for Mike to call. When a social worker answered the telephone, Mike made arrangements to visit the boys. After Mike arrived home, he seemed preoccupied. Finally, he said, "The boys asked if we'd take care of them, but we can't be temporary foster parents because they're living in a different state. The boys want us to adopt them!" After a lengthy silence, he asked, "What do you think?"

Contemplating the awesome responsibility, I answered candidly, "We can't…I can't. I'm sorry, Mike, but I've already raised two children through their teens. I don't have the strength to do it again. With their history, both boys will require enormous effort." Before he could speak one word, I continued, "You're either on duty or in court most of the time. I'm working and deeply involved in union business. One of our lives would have to change." Both sadness and guilt clutched at our hearts as we made a negative decision.

Now, it was four years later. Pedro was sixteen. He was calling to tell Mike that he had yet another change in address; then he added, "Daniel's in trouble. He's in jail!"

With remorse, I confessed to my diary: *I regret failing these boys.*

CHAPTER 55

Incidents (1990–1991)

March 1990: A robbery suspect, who had threatened his victims with a box cutter, was subdued into the back of a police cruiser. He kicked out the window of the black-and-white, so Mike had to aid another officer to forcibly place the suspect into a different cruiser. Mike once again reinjured his left knee, neck and right ankle. He also sustained another lumbar back strain.

January 1991: To complete a murder investigation, Mike worked eighty-five hours in one week. Most of the last sixteen hours were spent typing pages and pages—the entire case file. The next morning, Mike woke with a profusely swollen hand. We packed it in ice and used Vaseline to remove his ring. We drove to our ER where the doctor diagnosed carpal tunnel syndrome caused by excessive repetitive motion. Workers compensation denied the claim and refused to pay the ER bill.

CHAPTER 56

Capital Felony Murder (1991)

In September 1991, Mike and his partner were notified by their supervisor that a serious assault had taken place at 11 Madden Street, and they were the designated lead team. When they arrived members of the Field Service Division (uniformed officers) were still securing the crime scene. Officer Mark and Officer Daniel gave the following brief: While operating their cruisers, the sound of gunfire brought them to Madden Street, where they observed two Hispanic males shooting handguns at a third party. The patrolmen gave chase after the fleeing suspects. After a short volley of gunfire, the suspects were apprehended and placed under arrest. The victim was transported to the emergency room.

Hospital personnel could not save him. The next day, an autopsy was performed by the state medical examiner, who certified the cause of death to be the result of a bullet that had entered the victim's torso.

The "shut and closed" case seemed to be very simple, yet it required a lot of work because three separate investigation were necessary:

1. A police shooting investigation for the police officers.
2. A kidnap/murder investigation for the gunmen.
3. A capital/felony murder for the man who hired the killers.

Initially, physical evidence and several witnesses were located for both shooting scenes (the murder and the apprehension). Then three days later, Mike received a long-distance telephone call from the Bronx. A New York City lawyer was calling to explain that one of his incarcerated clients had contacted him about the Madden Street murder. Tim, his client, was serving time in the same correctional facility where the two accused assailants were being housed. In a direct conversation, those men not only claimed responsibility for the homicide but named the person who had hired them to rob and kill the victim.

September 26, 5:45 PM: Detectives Mike and Rose traveled to the jail to take a written statement. Unaware of Tim's friendship with the victim, the assassins had relayed the following information: They stayed at some girl's apartment when they arrived in town the night before the murder. In the morning, the two gunmen located the victim some distance from his home. At gunpoint, they forced him into his car and demanded he drive them back to his house. A struggle ensued in route, and Tim's friend, the victim, was shot while trying to escape his captors.

During a second conversation with the inmates. Tim learned that a Puerto Rican, named Eddie, was paying for the murder. Allegedly, no money had yet been exchanged. The assassins were to be paid after the job was done. When Tim heard that Eddie drove a Lincoln, he became suspicious about the identity of the contractor. He knew a man named Eddie who drove that type of car. Tim gave them Eddie's description and Eddie's new address, which was a private house in the Bronx.

On October 1, 1991, both detectives returned to New York City to interview the attorney. The lawyer knew everyone involved. According to him, Eddie's own brother, Junior, had told the victim's family that Eddie was responsible for the murder. Allegedly, Junior warned them that anyone thinking about taking retaliatory action would also be killed.

Mike and Rose returned and canvassed a wide area around the crime scene. They found a woman who affirmed a friendship with the victim and showed her a picture of one of the gunmen. She said that she had recently seen him with the victim on two occasions. Once, they visited her apartment. At that time, the assassin had been driving a white Lincoln town car with a dark top. This linked the hit men to the owner of the car, the Bronx contractor. Based upon this information, the NYPD Records Division was used to construct three photo arrays. Each array consisted of eight color police photos of similar Hispanic males. On October 11, Tim identified each of the three men responsible for killing his friend.

The detectives then went about finding the girls with whom the killers had stayed the night before the murder. Finally located, each was interviewed separately, and each one confirmed that three parties arrived in a white Lincoln town car with a blue top. All spent the night in their apartment on Hood Street, but when they awakened Sunday afternoon, the men had already left. Both young women were shown the three photo arrays at separate times. Both picked number 56 from photo array no. 1 and photo number 41 from array no. 2. From the last array, they identified Eddie and indicated that he was the one driving the Lincoln.

During the course of the investigation, Rose and Mike also located two eyewitnesses who could describe the victim's abduction from Jeffery Street at 11:00 AM on September 22, 1991. This information also verified Tim's statement.

October 22, 1991: The investigators once again traveled to New York City. This time they sought help from Precinct Forty-Six in the Bronx. They wanted to learn the identity of Eddie's brother, known only to them as Junior. Their search of NYPD records found an interesting case. Another convicted murderer had given a statement about being paid by three men: Eddie, Jesus Jr. and "Dopey". Records confirmed that their Eddie also had a brother nicknamed Junior. Photo array no. 4 was constructed.

While in the Bronx, Mike and Rose went to Eddie's home address. They observed the 1986 Lincoln town car with a white bottom and blue top. This was the same vehicle at the lady's apartment, and the same car seen in the vicinity of the homicide.

The investigation had to be put on hold for a month while Mike recuperated from injuries sustained in an unrelated case. This case was resumed on December 3. At 1815 hours (6:15 PM), Mike and Rose interviewed a brother of the deceased. Ramone's written statement relayed, "When I heard my brother had been shot, Ted [another brother] and I left to see him. As we were leaving the Bronx, we saw Eddie on the opposite side of the highway, driving his white Lincoln back to New York."

Ramone further stated, "Three days after my brother's murder, Junior approached me. He said 'Eddie's acting crazy. He and two other guys robbed and killed your brother.' Junior warned me not to take any counter action because Eddie would have me killed too." Ramone added, "Eddie was well aware that my brother was carrying a lot of money from his used car business." (He did not mention the drug business.) Ramone then reviewed the photo arrays and picked out Eddie and Junior.

The affidavit dated December 4, 1991, began: "The undersigned affiants, Detective Rose...and Detective Michael...are members of the...Police Department and have been employed in this capacity for a combined total of thirty years. Presently, said detectives are assigned to the Crimes Against Persons Division. Their primary responsibility consists of conducting criminal investigations, assaults, sexual assaults, robberies, kidnappings and homicides. These investigators have conducted numerous criminal investigations that have led to arrests and convictions."

Such an introduction seems pontifical, but it was extremely important to give notice that the case was handled by experienced police personnel. That fact not only added credibility to the investigation. It also gave notice to any state prosecutor that he or she may rely upon the senior officer's testimony to be that of an expert witness. Actually, two state prosecutors (district attorneys) must review a case to determine its merit, and both must agree that it is a good case before sending a judge the request for an arrest warrant.

Mike's affidavit ends: "The undersigned respectfully petition the court to issue an arrest warrant for the accused, Edwardo...DOB 12/22/67, charging him in violation of General State Statutes 53a–54b." This investigation was finally complete.

My diary attests to my concern: *The contractor was not quite twenty-four-years-old! Criminals are getting younger while Mike is getting older!*

CHAPTER 57

Downfall (1991)

Unlike television, real detectives are not allowed the luxury of working on one case at a time. During his capital felony/murder case, Mike became involved in someone else's robbery case because he happened to be at his desk when an excited woman came into the detective division. She had just seen a man who resembled the assailant who had previously robbed her at knifepoint a few days earlier. The suspect had been out in a front yard when she happened to drive by.

About 9:00 PM, Mike and Detective Liz drove the victim back to the designated location in order for her to identify the young man. When they arrived, he was no longer outside. The victim was instructed to remain in the back seat of their plainclothes car while they went to the front door. As they were identifying themselves to the nineteen-year-old occupant, the victim's scream gained everyone's attention. As Mike turned toward the car to instruct the woman not to get out, she screeched and pointed to the doorway, "That's him. That's the guy!" As Mike was turning back to the accused, his face met a right hook. A left punch immediately followed. The suspect's response had been instantaneous! The surprising blows sent Mike two steps backward where he was awkwardly pinned against a porch chair. Mike's suit jacket had opened, exposing his service revolver. The assailant lunged for Mike's .38. Detective Liz tried to intervene by grabbing the muscular suspect about the neck and striking his head with her portable radio. Liz was repelled by a stunning backward headbutt, which crushed her glasses into her face. She dropped the police radio. The strong young man succeeded in pulling Mike's gun from its holster, but Mike held fast. As their fight propelled them into the house, Liz regained possession of her senses and the radio. She called in a "10-0" (officer in trouble). As she was doing so, Mike disarmed the lethal combatant. The .38 fell to the floor. Mike still had the young man in hand when a woman appeared and picked up his gun. Helplessly, he awaited the bullet, but she did not fire at him. Instead, she quickly left the room with it. (Later she would be identified as the mother of the accused.) Liz rejoined the altercation. With her help, one handcuff had been locked in place. While struggling with the second handcuff, they were unpleasantly surprised when the woman returned, accosting them from behind. She literally threw herself upon the backs of both detectives! The bedlam continued, Mike fighting the accused, and Liz engaging the female who was presently gripping Liz's hair with both hands.

By the time a cruiser's siren could be heard, the battle had ended. Mike and the assailant were in the kitchen. Mike's energy was spent! But even so, he lay upon the floor with his opponent stubbornly contained in a vice-grip headlock. Mike was holding this position when the first help came through the door. That female officer quickly assessed the situation and went to the aid of Detective Liz. When other policemen arrived, Mike released the mulish teen who continued to resist arrest. Two patrolmen had to take him down to the floor again in order to secure the second handcuff. (This young man already had an established criminal record, thus his vigorous effort to avoid being arrested again.) After both, mother and son, were secured into cruisers, officers found Mike's Smith & Wesson hidden out on the porch.

When a supervisor arrived, Mike was still sitting on the kitchen floor. He could not seem to catch his breath, and he was plagued with continuous coughing. The sergeant asked, "Are you okay?"

Between rasping breaths, Mike replied, "I really am getting too old for this shit!" He suffered injuries to his left hand, upper lip, arms, knees, nose and face. He would not be able to get up and walk away like cops do in the movies. This was real!

Detective Liz suffered injuries to her neck, nose, face and left arm. Both disheveled detectives were transported to the emergency room for treatment. Liz was released, but Mike was admitted for further observation because of chest pain and shortness of breath.

I answered the incessant bedroom phone at 12:30 AM. Mike was on the line, and he sounded a bit groggy. I immediately asked, "Have you been drinking?" Not awaiting a reply, I instructed, "Don't try to drive home. Where—"

Mike interrupted, "That's why I'm calling, I won't be coming home tonight. But I'm not drunk, I'm in the hospital. They want me to stay overnight for observation."

I immediately repented. "What happened?"

I patiently listened to his slurred synopsis, which ended with his directive, "I don't want you to drive into the city tonight. Come and get me in the morning."

I agreed, but only if he let me speak to someone in charge. I had to find out exactly what was going on! A nurse informed me that Mike would not be leaving the hospital in the morning.

He was being admitted to the Cardiac Unit for four days of monitoring. There was a concern that he may have had a heart attack, but I was not to worry as he was presently medicated and stable. He said Mike had complained about further tearing his left bicep, but Mike's biggest concern was more damage to his bad left knee, which had already sustained several previous police injuries and minor surgery. The nurse clarified that these injuries were of secondary concern. At the moment, a possible cardiac problem was of the utmost importance. I gave the nurse the name of Mike's orthopedic surgeon and asked that he be notified. I also asked him to tell Mike that I would make the trip to the hospital after I completed my morning school bus run. (Spare drivers were in short supply.) My estimated time of arrival would be between 10:00 and 10:30 AM. Before hanging up, I had his nurse promise to call me if there were any changes in Mike's condition.

Even though I was becoming an old trooper at this, I still could not get back to sleep. Instead, I packed the things Mike would be needing for the next four days. After that was accomplished, I did the housework that I would not have time for later that day. Finally, 6:15 AM arrived, and I was punching my time card. Even though tired, I was anxious to get the job done. I safely delivered 125 students to a high school, a junior high school and a grammar school. Having completed my thirty-mile school route, I quickly returned to the bus terminal to get my car. I had to drive another thirty miles to get to the hospital, and I wanted to get there as soon as possible.

I was at Mike's bedside when the orthopedic surgeon arrived. Mike's longtime acquaintance did a cursory check, then told Mike he would do necessary repairs at a later date. Dr. Gray instructed Mike not to worry about anything now. He even joked, "Mike, a bad arm or knee won't be of any importance if you're dead. Let's take care of first things first." At this point in time, the doctor would only prescribe an anti-inflammatory for the swelling. (Mike was already on pain and heart medication.) Dr. Gray did not want to tell Mike that his left bicep was torn beyond repair, and he certainly was not going to tell him about his knee. It had a soft tissue calcification. It also had loose and fragmented joint bodies. A simple orthoscopic operation would do no good. This time, Mike was in need of a total knee replacement.

As if this was not enough to worry about, a doctor confided to me that the lateral view of Mike's chest x-ray showed a spot on one of his lungs! (Was it a tumor? Tuberculosis?) It took a few days to get a CT scan of his thorax. A radiology specialist told me that the spot previously seen on the x-ray film was most probably caused from superimposed shadows from calcium deposits that had formed due to past injuries. What a relief! I had lied to Mike. I had told him that the scan was only necessary to provide a better look at his chest. Now, I could tell him the whole truth.

One week later, a thorough stress test did not trigger any arrythmia or coughing. The results were so good that doctors wondered if the episode was a heart attack. But since Mike's blood chemistry had been questionable, Mike was sent home with a prescription for nitroglycerin—just in case. He was instructed to rest a while longer so that his battered body could heal as best it could.

Even if the cardiologist could not find anything wrong, I soon did. Physical exertion immediately triggered spontaneous coughing and shortness of breath. Mike refused to consult the doctor. He declared, "It will go away." But this continuing problem would prevent intimacy for months.

Three weeks into his recuperation, Mike saw the orthopedic surgeon, who recommended a prosthetic knee joint. Having learned that it could not withstand the abuses of police work and that the department would have to retire him, Mike decided to live with the pain for as long as he could. On the fifth week, Mike returned to work to complete his capital felony/murder case. Coping with a partially functioning left bicep was not too great of a problem because Mike was right-handed, but his constant knee pain caused him great stress. Mike rejected my request to see the orthopedic doctor. He remained adamant about forestalling the inevitable.

Mike could not help but wonder if a more adequate response time to Liz's 10-0 call could have saved him from some of his current agony. When he made inquiries, he found an ironic answer for the delay—a new communication system. The department had been switching over to the new system that night. Unfortunately, only half of the officers in the North End District had been issued new radios. The other half were operating old radios on a different frequency. This situation required the North End dispatchers to monitor both frequencies simultaneously. Consequently, they missed Liz's 10-0.

A detective informed Mike about the oversight. He explained that his radio had picked up her SOS call. Because help was not ordered, he switched his radio to the South End frequency and told that dispatch unit about the emergency missed by the North End dispatchers; backup was finally sent. The very next day after Mike's incident, all shifts were held over for an extra half hour so that every officer could be equipped with the proper radio and instructed how to use it. Thus, the dispatchers returned to coping only with the normal chaos.

In my diary, I lamented: *At this point, Mike's bicep is declared to have 10-15% impairment. The left knee has 25-30% impairment. The neck injury continues to impair his right shoulder movement and is declared to be a permanent 25% impairment. Not only is he too old for this…he is also too worn.*

CHAPTER 58

Rogue Cop (1992)

Mike was summoned to the Intelligence Division and questioned about his 1991 investigation of a city detective, an undercover narcotics officer. Mike referred the FBI agent to his written report that was submitted at that time. Mike was told that his report was missing! Since the report could not be found, Mike was asked to provide a verbal review.

After Mike's dissertation, the FBI interviewer informed Mike that their case had originated because of a complaint made by a drug dealer who became furious when the cop confiscated his sports car for his own personal use. (This was not Mike's investigation.) Their investigation had uncovered more than sufficient data to charge the undercover detective with massive grievances. They now wanted to add Mike's informant to their case, but Mike believed there was no reason to endanger his innocent source. He refused.

Mike's captain disagreed. He threatened, "You could find yourself in jail for withholding information."

Mike drawled, "I don't think so. My information didn't come from a paid informant. It came from a witness who is a good citizen, seeking no gratuity." Mike was only obliged to reveal a paid informant. It would take a judge's order to force him to reveal a well-intentioned citizen. If such a mandate were issued, Mike would have to decide whether or not to comply. Silence would protect his friend but send Mike to jail.

The interview had turned into an interrogation! Mike left the room, shaking his head. "Unbelievable!" He thought, *I'm the good guy, but I'm the one being threatened with jail!*

At the next parley, the FBI was once again in attendance. This time Mike informed them about the impounded drugs that had been stolen from the police department's secured lockup area. When Internal Affairs was notified about the missing evidence, they consulted the chief. Since it appeared the theft had been an inside job, this very serious matter was handled with complete secrecy. Mike was chosen to stake out the evidence room. Nothing again happened, so his covert assignment ended.

The informant, who was sought by the Feds, had approached Mike a few months after the internal theft. Mike received a telephone call from a concerned citizen. Mike knew the caller. He had known and respected him for several years. This man had started a private business, worked very hard and got his family out of the ghetto and into their own home. This friend was now relaying information about a city police officer allegedly involved in illegal drug activity! The businessman wanted to stop this bad cop from selling drugs to a family member, and he wanted to get this rogue off the streets. Mike was also told that the city detective had a partner who was a state police officer! Mike knew both men as undercover cops who did work together as partners on a regional narcotics team that worked statewide. Mike hoped that these cops were only working some kind of undercover sting. That hope faded when his friend said that these two cops were using their position to rip off drug dealers and then sell the dope themselves. Mike's first thought had been, *Shit! It's bad enough that I have to investigate police shootings, now this friend expects me to become another Serpico!* A little voice in his head said, *Just tell him you'll look into it.* But Mike knew in his heart that he would really have to follow up on this information. A dirty cop made every officer look bad, and that made every good cop's job that much harder. Mike decided not to tell anyone about it—not until he could substantiate his friend's statements.

Since Mike had established a rapport, and even friendships, with many people in the inner city, it was to those people he went in search of the truth. They entrusted Mike with information that led him to a named location. There, he sat alone waiting to see if the officers' car would arrive. John's plainclothes car did pull in, but that did not make him guilty. Mike thought about the many times he had to play games with criminals to solve a case.

Other people (including more of his friend's family) also contacted Mike, and their confirmations gave credence to the allegation. After further observation, Mike was convinced that something was wrong. He had to notify his division commander.

The commander officially assigned Mike to continue his investigation and arranged an exclusive meeting with the brass. Only the elite, the chief and his division commanders (Vice and Narcotics, Investigations and Intelligence) were in attendance. Mike recalled, "I felt like shit, but I knew my information was good." At the conclusion of the meeting, the commander of Vice and Narcotics suggested Mike work the case alone. He explained that Mike had proven trustworthy by bringing the situation to their attention. Since secrecy was essential, he did not want one of his own narcs to investigate John. Mike almost preferred not involving another detective, yet he was a bit leery about being the only one sticking his neck out. If his investigation could not prove the allegation, he would be buried into obscurity. If he were successful, there could be another problem. The results could be easily buried. Mike was not allowed to complete his investigation. After only one week, the commander of Vice and Narcotics declared, "The case is going nowhere, and I personally don't feel one of my own men could be guilty of such an atrocity."

Mike wrote his final report. It concluded with the declaration, "Further investigation is needed." After submitting it, Mike rationalized, "Fuck it. My hands are tied."

Shortly after that, John was reassigned to the Investigation Division! Mike was very surprised to find him working in his unit, but thought, *Oh well, at least they took him out of "narcotics". I'll keep my mouth shut, but no one had better assign me to work with him!*

A confrontation occurred between them in March. At 8:45 PM, Mike prepared to depart from his division for the streets. Two other detectives awaited him, and a third detective was seated at his appointed desk. As Mike walked past an empty desk, he noticed a wallet unattended. Because strangers were constantly coming in and out, he lifted the wallet into the air and asked, "Whose wallet is this?" (He intended to leave it in the sergeant's office should it not belong to anyone present.) His question was answered by John's resounding yell, which penetrated through the glass windows of an adjacent office. "It's mine, you fucking asshole!" Mike dropped the wallet back onto the desk and started walking toward the exit. With each step, John's profanity continued to assail him. The office door was thrown open, and the enraged detective strode after Mike.

With great restraint, Mike responded, "Sorry, I didn't realize it was yours." (At all costs, Mike had to avoid an altercation with this officer—not only because fighting with peers was forbidden, but because of Mike's secret investigation of him.) Mike had to choke back a snide rebuttal. He could not utter the disparaging thought that had immediately entered his mind. Mike could not say, *Don't worry, I'm not interested in your stash.* By voicing such a rebuke, Mike would reveal to this fellow officer that he was suspected of doing wrong. If the department was still keeping an eye on him, Mike did not want to be the one to give him any warning. So once again, he turned away and began walking toward the door. Apparently, John was not appeased. He picked up an office chair, prattled more vulgar comments, and swung the heavy metal object directly at Mike's head. Mike was saved from the blow only because the projectile had been thrown off-course when the bottom half of the chair fell off during midswing. It missed Mike by a few inches. Now, irate with the broken chair, the accosting officer threw its remnants to the floor. Then he came face to face with Mike and promised, "I'm going to kick your ass."

Mikes fists clenched, but he garnered utmost self-control by mutely repeating, *Don't hit him! Don't hit him!* With a deadly calm, Mike corrected, "You're the asshole. You can't kick my ass. You may be bigger but I'm crazier." While the real madman pondered these remarks, Mike left. The perplexed detectives who had witnessed the confrontation finally asked, "What the hell was that all about?"

Mike merely replied, "I guess he doesn't like me." But Mike had to ask himself that very same question. "Had John found out he was being investigated? How? Only the chief and three other high-ranking officers were supposed to know about it." (Much later, Mike would learn that the narcotic's commander had spoken to John's new sergeant in the Investigation Division. He had warned the sergeant to keep an eye on his new appointee. Afterward, the sergeant had allegedly told John, "You'd better watch your step." Whether this had been done to alert him or to straighten him out, Mike was never sure.)

A half hour after the confrontation, Mike had been willing to let the whole thing drop. But, after some thought, he decided it best to write a report—telling his side about the attempted assault. His statement not only described this incident but also a previous encounter. Five weeks before, John had exploded for no apparent reason but had apologized moments later—changing his personality 180 degrees. (His erratic behavior resembled that of a drug user.) Mike also divulged the fact that he had not been the only target. Recently, John directed unwarranted hostilities toward other peers as well. Mike ended his report, stating, "I regret having to write this complaint but do so in order to provide necessary documentation. The situation requires immediate attention, before anyone suffers bodily injury."

Mike received a **formal reprimand** from a sergeant who was unaware of the underlying circumstances. This really galled Mike. He felt that he had handled the situation admirably! He sent an appeal to the assistant chief asking vindication from the charge: Violation of Article II, Code of Conduct (using violent, abusive or profane language with the intent to incite another employee). Mike petitioned: *This writer feels the charge is unwarranted. As documented within my report, this detective's question "Whose wallet is this?" was what incited Detective John to physical violence. These words were not violent, abusive or profane. Detective John's attempt to do this detective bodily injury was unsuccessful only because the bottom of the chair fell off before contact could be made.*

Only after John's attempt did this detective make the statement. "You're the asshole." This detective's further statement, "You can't kick my ass," did not incite Detective John. It defused him and the situation. I maintain that I am only guilty of professional restraint and of writing a formal complaint in the hope of getting Detective John some help.

Now, almost a year later, he was explaining his investigations to the FBI agents. Mike informed them that if his police department could not find his original 1991 report, he would search his own files for a copy. He wanted to assure the Feds that he was not part of any cover-up. When the FBI notified the police department that Mike could produce a copy, the original was miraculously found. Mike was never again contacted about it, nor was he further pressured to disclose his original informant. Mike was not surprised. He was sure that the department's silence was not for the protection of his witness but for their own protection. Pushing the issue would spread the knowledge that his department had not cleaned their own house a long time ago.

Even though the FBI's evidence was more than sufficient to arrest John, they did not yet do so. Mike and I had to continue simmering in silence as the FBI continued their investigation. (They wanted to get everyone involved.) Finally, in 1993, John, the state trooper and four civilians were arrested. John was charged with fourteen counts: the intent to sell narcotics, sale of narcotics, robbery, conspiracy to sell drugs, possession of drug paraphernalia, burglary, kidnapping, attempt to commit robbery, larceny, attempt to commit larceny, attempt to commit burglary, attempt to tamper with physical evidence and racketeering.

Mike openly shared his mixed emotions with me. On one hand, he was glad that his suspicion would finally become proven fact; but on the other hand, he was unhappy that a fellow officer was being so openly persecuted for "losing his way". (Bad cops made sensational news.) I found myself assuring Mike, "John is responsible for his own predicament. After all, thousands of police officers are daily placed in tempting situations, but they remain steadfast upon an honest path." Law-abiding citizens have no idea of the temptations that constantly arise.

Diary notation: *The reprimand for Mike's alleged violation of the code of conduct had remained in Mike's personnel file for two years. It was finally removed.*

CHAPTER 59

Addiction (1992)

The year 1992 was the year that drugs became a part of my life. Our daughter called very early—before I left for work! She needed to know if I would be free after my morning school bus run. Her troubled tone inspired me to fib, "I have no plans. I'll be home around nine o'clock, I don't have to leave for my midday route until eleven o'clock. What's up?"

Lori's voice quivered as she spoke, "Gerald called around two o'clock this morning from City Hospital. He signed himself into the drug rehabilitation clinic!"

Instinctively, I covered the mouthpiece so that she could not hear the expletive that I directed at my son-in-law. Lori sounded as though she was about to break into open sobs, so I searched for something positive to say. I took in a deep breath to calm my anger and managed, "Well, it seems that he's found the courage to admit a starling truth! This certainly explains his mood swings. Seeking help is a positive step."

The sound of a filling tissue was evident before Lori asked, "Can you bring me to the hospital to pick up my car?"

"Of course, and I'll keep the kids for an hour. That way you can go in and speak privately to the doctor. What are you going to tell the children?" (I had to know how to answer their questions.)

Lori replied, "I don't want them to be worried. I'm going to send Sherrelle off to school just like a normal day. Her father goes to work before she gets up, so she won't miss him until supper time. When we get to the hospital, I'll just tell Spencer that his dad hasn't been feeling well, and the doctor wants to do some tests." That explanation would do for the three-year-old, but the oldest was in kindergarten and very astute. By evening, Lori would have a better idea of the situation and, hopefully, know how to handle it.

The good news was Gerald's health insurance would cover his medical expenses. The bad news was his masonry job offered no sick time. No work, no pay. The worst news was rehabilitation from crack took a very long time. The nurse explained that addicts of this substance usually fail the first time, many fail the second, some fail the third and others can never stay clean.

Well, this was a beginning! Gerald would be spending four days in hell—the initial withdrawal period. Then he would be sent to a well-known drug rehabilitation facility for a period of one month. This meant a minimum five weeks with no income! My concern was duly noted: *Thank God Mike and I are in a position to help, but what happens if his employer won't take him back?*

Drug addiction did not just hurt him, but our entire family. Lori was disillusioned and frustrated. The children felt insecure and frightened. Mike was livid. Lonny and Lisa were embarrassed, and I found myself numbed by the cruel irony. I wrote: *My son has become a narcotics detective; my son-in-law has become an addict! Turmoil lies ahead!*

In February 1993, the court awarded sole custody of Sherrelle and Spencer to Lori. The nurse had been right. Even though we had lent Gerald both moral and financial support, he still relapsed. He abandoned his family for drugs.

CHAPTER 60

Blue Flu (1992)

In early summer, a Blue Flu epidemic spread throughout the police department. Mike was one of the absentee policemen. He was still listed as injured, but if he were active, he would have probably been one of those officers calling in sick.

We were informed by a 6:00 PM news editorial. The station manager pronounced the police "sick-out" to be an irresponsible strike. Why? To protest the arrest of a police officer who had recently been arrested for assault. The officer claimed that he had to use force to make the arrest after the subject reached for the officer's gun. Had the station manager done any research, he would have discovered that the policeman's arrest was only one of many causes. The "sick-out" was, in fact, the only antidote available to police who were seriously ill from daily ingesting crime's toxic residue.

The mayor was the source of the most debilitating poison. Her boastful rhetoric spewed a stench that sent logical minds running for gas masks. In a TV interview, she gave herself credit for the officer's arrest (obviously utilizing the free publicly). She made this lethal proclamation, "This arrest shows that no one is above the law." Clearly, her innuendo left no doubt that she believed the officer guilty. Yet never did she voice such opinions about brutal gang members. Why not say, "The situation is sad. I wish to withhold further comment until after the allegation has been adjudicated." No, not her. She saw the incident as an opportunity for political gain! She hopped aboard the bandwagon, which was speeding across the nation. After the Los Angeles riots, the nation's news media went into a frenzy about bad cops.

Two days later, the mayor's publicity stunt backfired. NBC picked up the story and broadcast to the entire nation that her city was experiencing a 40 percent absentee rate in the police department. This indicated that she had lost control, and it was being nationally televised!

Astonishingly, the local station continued its stance, so I took pen in hand in an attempt to prove to the manager that his hasty diagnosis was faulty:

> *Sir,*
>
> *In regard to the Blue Flu, the arrest of one officer and the firing of another are indeed distasteful doses, but it is the mayor's rank politics which is totally unpalatable! In addition to this, you over-looked several other cankers which I am listing below:*
>
> *1. An Uncaring Administration: As the police officer has a responsibility for the safety and well-being of the public, so too, the administration has a responsibility for the safety and well-being of its police officers. Instead, administrators endanger officers by allowing positions to go unfilled, by threatening layoffs, and by issuing procedural mandates which leave police defenseless.*

*And when those officers are injured, they are thrust into political purgatory as they fight city hall for payments of their medical bills. I have first-hand knowledge of the administration's lack of responsibility. My husband's surgical bills are four months old; his prescriptions and medical supplies must be paid out of his own pocket because both the drugstore and the surgical supply company refuse to wait for compensation payments. They are too slowly sifted through the city's government bureaucracy. I have personally discovered that reimbursement is possible in only 4 to 5 weeks if the medical receipts **bypass** city hall and go directly to the compensation insurance company.*

Convalescing officers remain forgotten until their salaries become detrimental; then the administration washes its hands of those who must continue to endure partial disabilities. Positions as a dispatcher, a front desk concierge, an office clerk, a public liaison, a trainer, or even a worker in another city department are no longer offered. New policy forces the officer to engage in the futile task of seeking other employment with a resumé denoting him/her as an ex-cop with a pre-existing medical condition.

It is no wonder police officers dislike any conditions which unnecessarily jeopardize their health. Because my husband did adhere to the passive role mandated by this administration, he has suffered both physical pain and financial stress. Since he allowed himself to be injured first, the mayor should be happy. I am not! I am the one who renders him care and is awakened nightly by his moans of pain when he tries to find a more comfortable position. My son is now a policeman and my advice to him is "PROTECT YOURSELF."

2. An Unsympathetic Justice System: *The justice department has been lax in both the pursuit of charges and the dispensing of punishment for criminals who have injured police officers. The idea that injury is just a part of the job has become a blasé attitude. Unfortunately, I have first-hand knowledge of this as well. A judge recently refused to include my husband's injury charges in a robbery case. The judge stated that the two crimes should be tried as separate incidents, but an assault charge on behalf of the officer never did materialize. Why? Certainly, police injury is to be expected, but surely not condoned!*

A jury is not allowed any knowledge of a criminal's past arrest record; nor are they privileged with any statistics about past convictions. Yet, repeat offenders are responsible for a very large part of an officer's workload. Consistency is needed in sentencing. Career criminals should receive mandatory sentences. This would prevent coddling from judges who are too lenient, and justice would be equally dispensed.

3. A Negative News Media: *Heaven forbid the news media acknowledge or accept any responsibility for a bad situation. Never do* *they show the admirable side of police work. No coverage is given to the hundreds of dedicated cops whose enormous arrest records are never made public. Strides made by liaison officers and community groups are seldom mentioned. Unless sensationalism is involved, no one ever hears about the help given to grateful victims or their families.*

False reasons for not releasing information are:

    a.   *Crime figures would damage the city's image.*

    b.   *Releasing MOs would encourage copycat crimes.*

    c.   *No one is interested in such news.*

Forget the excuses. Withholding information has done nothing to reduce crime. Properly released information about crime being fought would generate some relief to frightened citizens. Knowing that the blue rank and file are dedicated to their protection would promote a more positive attitude. This would help both police morale and public morale. Good news would be appreciated.

    4.   ***The Silence of the Law-Abiding Majority****: Too many citizens feel that neither their opinion nor their actions can make a difference. Therefore, they remain silent. I assure you that both private and public communications of thanks would be gratefully received. Numerous communiqués need to be sent to city administrators, judges, prosecutors and legislators. Silent*

*voices must become a mighty chorus expounding,
"Enough is enough! Don't make deals with the
criminals. Render justice for the victims."*

*Those willing to contribute more than
voiced opinions may join a Neighborhood
Crime Watch, testify as friendly witnesses, fulfill
their jury obligations, petition to change laws
and vote to oust irresponsible public servants.*
<u>*With such action, citizens and police officers
can become a law enforcement team. When this
happens, the premise "police vs public" is no longer a successful weapon for a criminal's use.*</u>

My ire was so great that I sent copies of this letter to the
TV station, the radio station, the newspaper office and the city
council! My diary contemplation: *My diagnosis will never be
confirmed if others are not willing to discard the current popular
theory—cops are the bad guys. Because of this, officers often question if all their good deeds are for nothing. They wonder if anyone
appreciates their courage, their dedication, their pain or their personal sacrifices. Their symptoms: agitation, irritation, frustration,
apathy, humiliation and depression. These are only the symptoms;
not the causes of the virus which is the Blue Flu. I fear this virus is
extremely contagious, for even though Mike is not there, not directly
exposed, both of us are affected.*

It took some time, but television stations began to air more
documentary cop shows. Reimbursement for medical expenses
improved. The justice department allowed suits for police injury.
Mandatory sentencing was enacted. Repeat offenders could be
tried as career criminals. Good citizens began to openly reject
the premise that there is no such thing as a good cop. A new
concept, community policing, was being considered.

CHAPTER 61

A Blessing in Disguise (1992)

Mike had been working with his damaged knee for five months. Now, he was ready to concede the necessity of a total knee replacement. He certainly did not want to leave the police department, but his excruciating pain left him no choice. Once again, Mike's name was placed on the injured list, and he began presurgical therapy to prepare the muscles and ligaments for a new artificial left knee joint. After a month of extensive therapy, Mike reached the therapist's goal (a ninety-degree bend). He made two autologous blood donations so that he could be transfused with his own blood during surgery. The surgery date was getting close.

A few nights before, I watched intently as an educational cable channel broadcast the entire surgical procedure. Mike's incision would be about ten inches long, starting above the knee and trailing dead center down below. The femur (above the knee) and the tibia (below the knee) had to be exposed. To extricate the knee joint, a portion of both bones would be sawed away. At their severed ends, the exposed center marrow would be slightly hollowed to accommodate the metal replacement shafts. The doctor would hammer these metal dowels into place, much like fitting pegs into holes. The upper and lower bones would then be reconnected by a modern plastic joint. Mike's own patella (kneecap) would be reused, but shavings from its underside would first be retrieved to make the glue needed to secure it to the artificial joint. How simple! How complex! It was a good thing Mike had decided not to watch the procedure before surgery. I, however, benefited from the lesson because it gave me warning about what was lying ahead.

When Mike was returned to his room, I was surprised to see that a drain had been connected from the surgical site to a recycling intravenous machine. Mike was literally transfusing himself with his own lost blood. I was also surprised that he was awake. As the anesthesia subsided, the pain escalated. Mike was in such agony that his blood pressure went sky-high. The floor nurse immediately placed a call to the surgeon; a half hour later, Mike was snoring from an added dose of morphine. (Over the years, Mike had taken so much pain medication that normal doses no longer worked on him.)

The next day, his leg was attached to a CPM torture machine. The hydraulic unit forced his knee into continuous motion for eight hours a day.

On the morning of his scheduled release, the doctor felt heat generating from Mike's knee and noticed a large swelling beneath. Apparently, the recycling machine had been removed too soon because Mike was still bleeding internally. The hemorrhaging blood was pooling behind his knee. Instead of going home, Mike was rescheduled for a return trip to the operating room. But none were available. All regular and emergency surgeries had to be completed first. So, we began our long wait. At 9:00 AM, Mike was once again hooked up to an IV bag and was restricted from any food or drink. At midnight, fifteen hours later, an orderly finally wheeled him into the operating room!

There he was given general anesthesia so that any forming scar tissue could be torn, the pooling blood could be suctioned, and the bleeder cauterized.

A few days later, Mike was released, vowing to never return to a hospital again. But torture was not yet over. At home, Mike was exercised on a CPM rental for eight hours a day for the next two weeks. A visiting nurse came every other day to manipulate his physical therapy, and I provided physical therapy four times a day. By the third week, we were taking trips to the hospital every other day for more physical therapy. During the months that followed, the shooting phantom pains (like those experienced by amputees) began to subside. Mike worked his way from a walker, to crutches, to a cane, to a limp. It took a long while before he could say, "Look, honey, I can almost fake a real walk."

One of Mike's friends had a total knee replacement, but his knee did not wiggle laterally. When Mike asked his surgeon about this, the arrogant man merely asked, "Do you want me to redo it?" He already knew Mike's answer!

At age fifty-two, Mike had to accept the fact that he could no longer be a part of the force. The only question was just how Mike would choose to end it. Should he take a disability or choose regular retirement? He had more than the twenty years required for retirement eligibility. As a retiree, he would have a chance to find other work. Labeled disabled would, however, give him tax-free money. Well, there would be a very lengthy recovery period in which to decide. In either case, Mike would sorely miss his beloved profession.

A diary page quotation: *How strange that someone else's robbery case would be the cause of Mike's demise. But even simple traffic stops have caused an officer's death. Mike has only lost a knee. Maybe this injury is a blessing in disguise. It is forcing him to leave law enforcement while he is still alive!*

CHAPTER 62

Federal Reprimand (1993)

Our next knowledge about the rogue cop was obtained from a city newspaper in 1993. The article was titled "Grand Juror Details Police Abuse." The article told about a federal probe that brought about six arrests. In regard to the two policemen involved, a judge openly placed responsibility upon local administrative personnel.

An excerpt from the judge's interim report states, "The ability of a rouge member of the Statewide Narcotics Task Force to operate illegally and unprofessionally with impunity for two years raises disquieting questions of supervision, control and absence of accountability checks for undercover police personnel."

My thought: *A public trial brought everything out into the open, and the integrity of honorable cops has again been sullied. Generalized criticism is such an unfair burden! A few officers may not handle it well. Some may find accusing citizens repulsive. But most officers will understand the dilemma and place the blame where it belongs, with "the Rogue".*

CHAPTER 63

It Ain't Easy (1994)

Between 1976 and 1983, Mike had fulfilled extra responsibilities. He had been a pro bono member of the board of
directors for the Police Benevolent Association, a non-union
society which supported <u>all officers</u> and their families in any
way needed. Mike served first as its secretary, then as its vice
president.

I also did volunteer work. For seventeen years, I logged
hundreds of hours doing union business, which assured the best
working conditions possible for two hundred <u>school bus drivers</u>
and mechanics.

My union involvement began when a former employer
appointed me to an established labor/management team. This
labor unit eventually evolved into a sanctioned private union in
which peers elected their own representatives; year after year, I
was one of the elected. For the drivers in my town, unity was
imperative. Our school department hired private companies to
transport thousands of children. Every few years, a new contract was awarded to the lowest bidder, and the drivers had to
seek work with the new company. By uniting, drivers could
maintain employment with a rollover policy that protected

their seniority and their benefits. Even though new management took over, the drivers remained the same. This guaranteed a smooth transition. I was president of our private union when a large international company won the bid in 1987. Deciding more expertise than mine would be needed, I brought my drivers to an international union. Since I had accepted a position as chief steward (without compensation), I continued to negotiate labor contracts with every succeeding company.

I also headed a safety committee that reviewed accidents and targeted danger areas (faulty equipment, yard maintenance, routing problems, working conditions). The committee also suggested training topics and followed up on children's discipline procedures.

I wrote many informative articles for the union's local newsletter. My article "Missing Social Security Benefits" was an exposé. I had discovered that employees had not received any social security credits for 1987 and researched corrective action. My query letter to the IRS initiated an investigation. Perhaps there is a bit of a detective in me too.

By the 1994–1995 school year, I was slowly beginning to delegate more and more of my responsibilities to others, but when someone needed help, I just could not refuse. So, many still approached me! Each would begin by saying, "I know you don't do this anymore, but…" Eventually, I disciplined myself not to become involved. Instead, I would recommend a steward who had expertise in the area of his/her concern. Mike was no longer involved with the PBA and often reminded me that I had more than fulfilled my responsibilities as well. I reminded myself that outside interests had, at one time, been a contributing factor causing our temporary separation. But I could not retire my position just yet! Another employer seemed to be intent upon testing several sections in the union contract, and several cases were being taken to arbitration. We won every labor dispute before I relinquished my position. Now, I merely serve as a consultant.

In late September 1994, the nightly television news had jumped on a story about a school bus driver being cited for speeding, a topic of great interest to thousands of parents who entrust their children to someone else. Of course, there had to be one proverbial bad apple in the basket, but this basket was a school bus containing a much more precious commodity. The situation was serious. During the rest of the week, anyone with even the most minute complaint brought it to the media: bus stops were too far from their houses, children were on the bus too long. (It was the school department who instituted a one-hour maximum ride.) Two-thirds of the buses had no monitors. Discipline was lacking. Drivers were not waiting for children to get to their bus stops.

Even though all policy was dictated by the school department, parents somehow held drivers responsible for fixing everything! Parental patience gave way, and a tenseness clouded the atmosphere. All the good done by most drivers on a day-to-day basis had become totally obscured, so I sought to provide a clearer view. I submitted an article to the newspaper. This was printed on the editorial page:

It Ain't Easy

> *To use an old colloquialism, "It ain't easy."*
> *Yet 190 city school bus drivers excel daily. It*
> *is unfortunate that their efforts go unnoticed.*
> *These drivers meet many challenges. Even*
> *normal routing requires extraordinary skill to*
> *manipulate 65, 71 and 77-passenger buses in*

and out of traffic and through side streets lined with parked cars. The first obstacle must be met in the dark when leaving the terminal. Each driver must pull out from a blind street onto a busy four-lane thoroughfare; and this must be done without the help of a traffic light, a police officer or even a warning sign for on-coming cars. Succeeding that, one's skills are further tested by road construction, wet leaf-covered streets, over hanging tree branches, malfunctioning traffic lights and fogged windows. Later protruding snow banks will further narrow streets and intersections; even worse, there will be ice!

Route changes are constant because of late enrollment, new addresses and the city's school of choice policy. Each change disrupts pick-up and drop-off time schedules previously established and causes inconveniences. Drivers then hear lamentations from unhappy parents. Consistent timing is also hindered by kindergarten students. Their parents often neglect to use identification tags, and many are often late to retrieve their child from his/her bus stop. (The school department insists that kindergarteners be met by a parent or authorized responsible party.) The driver must then return a half-day child to his/her school at mid-day. A full-day student goes to an emergency drop-off center in the PM. (The parent is then responsible for retrieving their child.)

Individual safety is another enormous challenge. This encompasses a barrage of respon-

sibilities: changing unsafe stops, identifying strangers at bus stops, tying up shoelaces, making sure pens and pencils are inside backpacks, instructing children to hold umbrella points down, confiscating weapons, keeping children seated, settling disputes and maintaining general discipline (often without a monitor). There must be constant reinforcement of Thumper's Rule: "If you can't say something nice, don't say anything at all."

Paperwork must be completed daily. This includes: inspection circle checklists, monitor's pay cards, DDR forms for vehicle maintenance, incident reports for discipline, dead-stop notices, child abuse reports, traffic violation forms for cars passing through flashing school lights and hopefully, not an accident report or injury verification.

Good drivers provide not only physical comfort but psychological support as well. This must be adequately rendered (not too much; not too little). A hug is not permitted, but encouraging conversation is a must. Hopefully, only simple first aid for a bloody nose or scraped knee will be required, but one never knows.

In order to eliminate unnecessary challenges, the Driver's Safety Committee has made the following requests of the school department:

1. *All principals receive updated policy so that standardized discipline be enforced at every school.*

2. *All bussed students receive the Bus Conduct—Student Agreement Form.*
3. *All kindergarteners be sufficiently tagged.*
4. *A comprehensive safety training program become a part of a standardized evacuation drill.*
5. *Pictured identification cards be issued to all junior and senior high school students which identify the student by name and by the bus number to which they are assigned.*
6. *A police liaison officer be available throughout the entire PM routing time.*
7. *Drivers be given a list of students' names listed by stops.*

The job of a school bus driver certainly isn't easy, but those dedicated people get the job done, day-in and day-out, no matter what the challenges are!

At the end of the 1993–1994 school year, the school department had agreed that all these requests had merit. By the end of the 1994–1995 school year, only half of those requests had been implemented. I vented my frustration to my diary: *Changing a bureaucracy is almost impossible. Almost... They do not know how tenacious I can be, especially about the safety of children, even when they are not my own.*

CHAPTER 64

Costly Success (1994)

Mike's perseverance brought him great success. During his police career, he was involved in approximately 300 homicide investigations, and he was a lead investigator in about half of those. All but two of his cases culminated with successful prosecutions. The two exceptions implicated **politicians**, and both cases abruptly ended when Mike's requests for warrants were denied! Even though Mike knew who committed one murder and who paid for the other, there had been no closure. Because there is no statute of limitations for murder, Mike still hopes that another detective will someday succeed in obtaining justice for the victims.

Mike's incredible record as a lead detective is best described in his own proud words, "I'm Plus Two!"

How so? You ask? You just did some quick math and you figured, "He's minus two."

Extraordinary cold cases must be considered. Mike was assigned to review unsolved murder cases. He was allowed to choose any case and any partner. They solved not only one inactive case, but four cold cases. These bonus cases allowed him to grade his career as "Plus Two." He still felt like he could have been a "Plus Four" if prosecutors had not chosen to exercise **extreme caution** with his two political cases.

Mike prolonged his total knee replacement for as long as possible. Once done, he spent months on the injured list. When doctors declared him to be recuperated, the police department deemed Mike unfit for duty. He technically remained an employee of the police department while he used up his accumulated holidays, vacation time and sick leave. The Workers Compensation Commission acknowledged several permanent injuries, which were enough to designate Mike "disabled". But Detective Mike took a regular pension! He did not want to be labeled disabled for future employment. On September 19, 1994, it became official. Mike was relieved of his duty on the blue line.

Was our sojourn over? My diary reflects: *Is my life finally free of fear? Not quite. Mike may still be in jeopardy. He has knowledge about murderers still at-large. I remind myself that his documented case files serve as his protection. Any foolish act perpetrated against him would cause those files to be re-opened. It's more likely that Mike's own medical files will be the ones to be re-opened.*

CHAPTER 65

"Slam-Banger" (1995)

"Slam-Banger" is an affectionate name for an easily solved case because both the victim and the perpetrator are quickly identified. Even though easily solved, it may not be quickly closed. When perpetrators flee, it takes a great deal of investigation to apprehend them. Sometimes these criminals disappear and remain fugitives for years.

For instance, back in August 1988, a man had been murdered. His head was both struck by a rock and clubbed with a board while his chest was stabbed by a buck knife. On September 26, 1988, arrest warrants were issued for two Jamaican males. It was not until December 1990 that one man was found in another state. He was extradited, stood trial and found guilty. The second assailant remained a fugitive until July 1995. He had been arrested in the south on unrelated charges, but thanks to the world of computers, his outstanding murder warrant popped up during a routine check. Now, seven years later, he was being extradited and would finally stand trial for the murder.

By this time, Mike had been out of police work for ten months. He thought he was done with it until a superior court subpoena arrived. It summoned him to testify about this old case. To prepare, he went to the station to thoroughly review his case file (August 19, 1988–September 21, 1988).

August 19, 1988:

At 1910 hours (7:10 PM), a patrol unit was dispatched to Hunter Street in reference to a serious assault. The patrolmen found one black male, leaning over another black male who was lying on the lawn. Since he was suffering from apparent stab wounds, they called an ambulance, secured the crime scene and notified the detective bureau.

At 1915 hours (7:15 PM), investigators arrived as EMTs were rendering medical assistance to the unconscious victim. The street sergeant briefed the detectives. Based upon the initial information, the victim and the black male had been walking south when they were approached by a Jamaican male bearing a knife. An argument began. The Jamaican was yelling, "Where's my stuff? You ripped me off." The assailant summoned two more Jamaicans to participate in the assault. Fists, rocks, a board and a knife were used. After the assault, all three perpetrators went down to the apartment building at 50 Hunter Street, but they soon came back out and fled away in a car. Tom, the second black male was also assaulted, but he was able to assist his friend out of the street.

Detective Mike and Detective Ali then spoke to Tom. He identified the stabbed victim as E.S.; then stated, "We were walking down the street when a Jamaican came over, waiving a knife and shouting at my friend. The guy spoke Jamaican dialect, so I didn't understand the entire conversation. I think he was yelling about a woman. My friend was giving him directions to a place on Hunter Street when another Jamaican arrived, took the knife from the first guy and began jabbing it at E.S. I was fighting with a third man, when the first guy came back with a board and hit E.S. in the head. Later, the guy I had been fighting with got into a Regal or a Cutlass parked up the street and dove the other two men away."

Another eyewitness said she had spoken to one assailant just before the incident. She relayed that she had previously seen him in the second-floor window at 50 Hunter Street.

At 1935 hours (7:35 PM), Mike and Ali spoke to an ER doctor who pronounced the victim dead, apparently from a stab wound to the chest. Another laceration was on his left side. They returned to the station to further interview Tom.

August 20, 1988:

At 0502 hours (5:02 AM), detectives obtain a search warrant for the second-floor apartment (1B) on Hunter Street where they believed the perpetrators resided. Several items were seized into evidence. 1.)

Identifying documents (family and personal photos); 2.) a substantial amount of narcotics; 3.) money.

At 1000 hours (10:00 AM), an assistant state medical examiner performed an autopsy and certified the cause of death as a homicide due to a stab wound to the chest.

At 1345 hours (1:45 PM), investigators ascertained the name of one of the apartment's occupants. Mike and Ali sought out his estranged wife. She identified a numbered photo taken from the apartment as her husband and verified that he currently looked exactly like the picture. She had last seen him two weeks prior. She also identified him in another photo in which he was wearing a gold chain with a unique medallion.

At 1910 hours (7:10 PM), a male witness came into the police station and was shown a photo array. He picked out one of the Jamaican males who had struck the victim.

August 23, 1988:

At 1100 hours (11:00 AM), Mike and Ali went to the home of a juvenile witness to re-interview her in the presence of her guardian. She confirmed that she had been in front of her home on Hunter Street and had witnessed an argument over drugs. She stated that a black male, dressed in blue (Tom), was fighting with a real short Jamaican male whom she identified in a photo array. From another array, she picked out the Jamaican who held both the knife and then a board. She said a funny nickname was printed on the gold medallion hanging from his necklace. She knew he lived at 50 Hunter Street.

August 24, 1988:

At 1145 hours (11:45 AM), a resident of apartment 1A was interviewed. She confirmed that several men, whom she did not know by name, lived in 1B where there was always a lot of traffic flowing in and out. From photo array no. 1, she identified the man with a funny nickname and another man who now had shoulder length, curly hair, unlike his police photo. From photo array no. 2, she identified the third man. (Police records indicated that all were in their twenties.)

At 1730 hours (5:30 PM), detectives re-interviewed the Jamaican female who had spoken to one of the assailants. She described him: dark complexion, short hair with one patch dyed red and a "pock-marked" face. She identified him in photo array no. 1. It was the Jamaican who first approached the two black Americans. He was yelling, "Where's my stuff?" The victim said, "I didn't take your stuff. I'll take you to the girl." At first, Tom did not get involved but began to walk along with them. Then the first Jamaican yelled to the other two. One had an odd name. From her viewpoint, she could see only "the little guy with the Jerry curls" fighting with the black Afro-American, wearing a blue shirt (Tom). She identified the Jamaican from a photo array and then relinquished the names of two other witnesses.

At 1940 hours (7:40 PM), another male witness specified that it was while the first Jamaican male was picking up a board, that the second Jamaican, the one wearing a gold chain with an animal's head, grabbed a rock and struck the victim's head. The third Jamaican only fought with the victim's friend. When they left the crime scene, all three walked right past this witness who stated the second Jamaican was holding the buck knife as he passed by. The witness identified all three parties.

At 1945 hours (7:45 PM), another male witness was re-interviewed. At first, he had been reluctant because he feared for his family, but he now confirmed the above account, adding the deceased had been brought to his knees by the second Jamaican before the first returned to strike his head with a board. He knew that the "fat guy" lived on Hunter Street and identified him from a photo array. He concluded by giving the detectives the name and address of another witness.

At 2000 hours (8:00 PM), this female witness verified the entire incident. Her story only deviated as to just when the victim had been struck with the rock.

At 2015 hours (8:15 PM), another female witness picked out the first and third Jamaicans from photo arrays.

August 26, 1988:

At 1437 hours (2:37 PM), a man and his girlfriend came to the police station to relate their knowledge regarding the murder on August 19, 1988. He stated that around midnight on August 17, 1988, his girl-friend entered the apartment. She nervously explained, "The Jamaican guy up the street is after us! E.S. and me tried to switch him a "bum bag". (They had switched a bag of cocaine with another filled with white powder.) He said he was surprised to hear that his girl had been hanging around with the victim because E.S. had once stolen property from him and was no longer welcome in his home. Angrily, he had told his girl-friend, "Don't bring that shit in here." But he relented and allowed her to stay. Fifteen minutes later, E.S. was ringing his doorbell and calling into the intercom for the girl. The boyfriend answered, "She doesn't live here." E.S. left, but his girlfriend remained hiding inside his apartment for the next three days.

In the late afternoon on Friday (August 19, 1988), a voice was once again on the intercom asking for the girl. The boyfriend could hear him arguing with the other men who had Jamaican accents, so he told his girlfriend not to ring E.S. into the building. Later he was awakened by his girlfriend screaming at his window. When he went over to the window, he saw the victim being helped out of the street. Then the police and the ambulance arrived. He stated, "It has taken me all this time to convince her to tell the police about her involvement."

She then gave her statement: "My girlfriend introduced me to E.S. a couple of months ago. Two days before he was murdered, I went with him to 50 Hunter Street, apartment 1B. We knew they sold drugs and we had this plan to steal a bag of cocaine by swapping it with a phony bag. When the Jamaican handed me his bag, I told him that $30 was too much and then handed the phony bag back to him. He realized what had happened and chased us. When he grabbed E.S., I was able to duck into my boyfriend's apartment (on the same street). I've been hiding ever since."

She confirmed that at approximately 7:00 PM on August 19, 1988, the victim and a Jamaican were once again seeking her at her boyfriend's address. She stated that E.S. was yelling into the intercom, "Help me. This guy's got a knife." Once again, she did not answer the door. She went to a window and watched as the Jamaican began fighting with the victim. She identified the Jamaican.

September 21, 1988:

At 1919 hours (7:19 PM), Ali and Mike contacted Tom to clarify some aspects of his voluntary statements, made on August 19. He insisted that there had been only one knife involved. The second Jamaican had taken the knife form the first man and then began poking it at his friend. Tom stated that the second Jamaican was with E.S. when he collapsed.

The man who had attacked Tom would be charged with assault, but what about the other two? Since this easy "slam-banger" had several witnesses, two murder warrants should be issued, right? Wrong! A murder conviction requires a jury to have *no doubt*. During the stabbing, Tom was engaged in a fight with the third Jamaican. A defense attorney would tell a jury that Tom's statement was merely conjecture because he did not see the knife enter his friend's body. Other witnesses would confirm that two men did have possession of the knife, yet none could testify that they actually saw the death blow. Since there was no way to prove which man was the actual killer, the only sure way to obtain a conviction was to issue two warrants that merely charged each man with **Accessory to Murder**. Mike had to accept the fact that some justice was better than no justice.

The next step was to find the assailants and make an arrest. It took two years to find one and seven years to find the other. So, you see, even a simple "slam-banger" can end with a twist!

Diary entry: *Thanks to Mike's meticulous case file and his expert testimony, the second fugitive was finally convicted in 1995. Case closed.*

CHAPTER 66

Rape (1995)

After retiring, Mike received a phone call from an assistant district attorney. She informed him that she had recently prosecuted someone Mike knew well. Vern, the bad penny, had been convicted for **rape**, **drug violations**, and **kidnapping**. His latest female victim was brave enough to pursue justice!

When Mike mentioned the rape case of 1978, the young prosecutor admitted she had no knowledge about it. This was understandable because there had been no prosecution. She was appalled to find that Vern's MO in 1978 was identical to her recent case. This time, Vern was sentenced to eighty-five years. At his age, it should mean a life sentence, even with early release as a factor.

My thought: *Justice has finally prevailed, but I wonder how many other victims there have been throughout the years?*

CHAPTER 67

A Change in Course (1995)

Mike had designated degrees of impairment for the left knee, right ankle, cervical spine, left bicep and ileostomy. But his innate work ethic had caused him to reject a disability retirement. He considered himself still capable of gainful employment, but it was more than a year and many resumés later before he finally found an employer who agreed with that assessment.

At the age of fifty-five, Mike went back in uniform! He was now a security guard. My diary entry exclaims my amazement: *Even with all of his ailments, he manages twelve-hour shifts. One may question, "Isn't this work demeaning?" The answer is "NO." Mike believes that any work is an honorable thing; and I admit, the added income is a **welcome supplement** to his police pension check.*

Your excursion into our lives will end when you reach the federal court house. There, an ordinary man is cordially greeting personnel by their first names. While his camaraderie is relaxed, his eyes are as sharp as the creases in his pants. A diary critique describes: *Mike's hair is now a distinguished white, clipped very short and neat. His salt-and-pepper mustache I keep precisely trimmed. The slight pink of his ears hints of hypertension. On the right side of Mike's face is a white pencil scar line. It begins at the edge of his hazel eye, extends across the temple and disappears into his hairline. His carriage depicts pride.*

Evidence of all other police injuries remains suppressed—hidden under clothing, skin and dental crowns. My keen eye notices negligible body stiffness and a very slight limp. Only you, the reader, will know about the extraordinary past of this obscure gentleman.

At the school bus terminal, you can still see me behind the wheel of a thirty-five-foot vehicle. Could anyone guess what I have experienced?

Mike and I have survived our trek through hell. Many couples did not. From a class of twenty-eight graduating cadets, we are one of the only two remaining married couples. Somehow, we found the courage to confront the many challenges that plagued us throughout our tour of duty. Now we are civilians, who are embarking upon our next journey—into senior years. As destiny's map continues to unfold, we hope it will reveal a hidden valley of peace.

EPILOGUE FOR MY GRANDCHILDREN

My primary goal in documenting our journey was to provide a map with which you could explore the mysteries of your family's route. During my writing, I began to ponder a secondary goal. Could publishing my work benefit others as well? Sharing our bumpy road with the general public might encourage compassion for all police families. It would be most rewarding, too, if our journey could provide naive cadets an informative trip into the field of law enforcement. Our personal conflicts may even serve as warning signals to detour other police couples safely around the hidden potholes.

For now, do I dare hope that I have opened your eyes, your minds and your hearts? Have I brought you to a new destination, a point where you can see that **everyone is more than they first seem**—even an ordinary security guard and a workaday school bus driver? I trust so, for new perceptions will prove to be enlightening, and you will understand why certain paths were taken.

Soon, you will be choosing your own way in life. Hopefully, our example sets you in the right direction. I await your choices with optimism.

All my love.
Nana

CPSIA information can be obtained
at www.ICGtesting.com
Printed in the USA
LVHW082141130420
653354LV00016B/269